A Disney

CHILDHOOD

Comic Books to Sailing Ships

A MEMOIR

by

CATHY SHERMAN FREEMAN

Cathy Sherman Freeman

BearManor
Media

Albany, Georgia

A Disney Childhood: Comic Books to Sailing Ships — A Memoir
© 2012 Cathy Sherman Freeman. All rights reserved.

Some names have been changed and a few sequence of events are out of order.

Published in the USA by:
BearManor Media
PO Box 1129
Duncan, OK 73534-1129
www.BearManorMedia.com

ISBN 1-59393-682-6

Printed in the United States of America

Design and Layout by Allan T. Duffin.

Table of Contents

Dedication

To My Father
George Ransom Sherman

To My Family
Brian, my husband, and my two smart funny children

To My Childhood Family
*My mother, Nancy Fenno Sherman Ford,
who was always up for an adventure,
and my three brothers, John, Jim and Jeff*

Chapter 1

Born into a Fantasy World

I was born into a fantasy world. Father was in charge of writing, editing and publishing comic books for Walt Disney Studios. Fairy dust flew rampantly through our house a short block from the Disney Studio. Wherever my imagination took me, I'd hang on for the ride. I ate ice cream for breakfast and believed trees could talk. What I couldn't foresee was the unexpected Foe waiting to strike. My life was fated as Sleeping Beauty was fated. My quest was how do I deal with fate? Charm it, resist it, ignore it, accept it? Do I keep quiet or expose it to the masses?

Impossible! Four white mice will never be four white horses. Such fol-de-rol and fiddle dee dee of courses. But the world is full of zanies and fools, who don't believe in sensible rules, and won't believe what sensible people say, and because these daft and dewey-eyed dopes keep building up impossible hopes, impossible, things are happening every day.

This was the song from *Cinderella* that I fell asleep to night after night. I was a young girl born in the 1950s and believed I was a long-lost princess just left on the wrong doorstep. I was secretly waiting for Prince Charming to claim me. The only foil in this scenario was that my three brothers told me time and time again I was no princess. I could compete with them at football, tennis, academics, and poker. Maybe the third of four children was a tomboy and not a long-lost princess after all.

My name is Mary Catherine, although I have always gone by my nickname, Cathy. I have brown eyes and blonde hair. My oldest brother is John, then Jim, and Jeff the youngest. We were four children born within five years of each other. We were pretty good friends and looked out for each other most of the time. I had my own room with shiny lime-green and bright pink flowered wallpaper. My three brothers shared one room that was once the master bedroom. My parents took the last bedroom in our three-bedroom house.

Father's first job at Walt Disney Studios was in 1952. He was an assistant to Joe Reddy, Head of Public Relations. This position developed into his handling the personal guests of Walt Disney himself. Father would give visitors a tour of the studio. He quickly became friends with Disney animators, writers, directors, and other personnel. He'd explain the unique animation camera that created 3-D effects before computers were invented. When Disneyland opened in 1955 he'd also escort guests there. Father even wrote an article for *Grolier Society Encyclopedia* on "The Production of Animated Cartoons."

After three years Father left Disney to try his hand at owning a business. He bought a small newspaper in Point Reyes, California, called The *Baywood Press*. He thought the work rewarding, the community charming, but the job was never-ending. He needed to write and edit the stories, create and sell ads, print and deliver the weekly paper all for 7 cents an issue. This didn't generate enough income to support the needs of his increasing family. In 1957, when a third child was on the way, me, he returned to Disney Studios. His new title was Head of Foreign Relations, which evolved into Head of Publications.

Father worked in an office on the second floor of the ink-and-paint building. This building had been designed with an advanced air-conditioning system in order that the paints used on animation cels could dry slowly. There was a tunnel connecting Father's building to the animation building to ensure no rain fell on the original animator's artwork being transported back and forth. This tunnel was also used as an air raid shelter during World War II when the threat of Japanese invasion dominated the minds of most Californians. There was a basement nicknamed "the morgue," where artwork was stored after it was filmed. The buildings were brick with pathways and grass lawns that had the feel of a college campus. It was an inviting atmosphere for staff and visitors.

From my birth people from all over the world visited our house. Disney representatives, writers, illustrators, and distributors would gather and socialize during the afternoons in our living room or on the outside porch. The children were just "part of the crowd." We weren't put on stage but we were included, allowed to sit with the grown-ups and listen. Listen to stories from people who lived halfway around the world. Listen to how their lives were so different from ours yet so much the same. Hear about a fruit that was explained patiently as we asked many questions. We wanted to know what it looked like, smelled like and tasted like. Why didn't we have any in our supermarkets? I'd never seen a fruit that when sliced looked like a starfish but tasted like a mixture of apples, melons and lemons. We tried to visualize this starfruit and dreamed of tasting it.

Another treat was the day, once a month, when Father would come home from work and pull from his leather briefcase four hot-off-the-presses Disney comic books. We'd fight over who got to read the *Uncle Scrooge* one first. If there was a *Beagle Boys* we'd grab that second. Our least favorite was *Chip and Dale*. It wouldn't be long before this set of comics would be tattered and torn, and we'd be eagerly waiting the day Father came home with a new batch.

When I was seven, Father started inviting me to come to work with him to help screen comic book story submissions. I would be given a pillow on the floor and a large stack of typed manuscripts containing potential comic book stories to read. These were typed on flimsy onion-skin paper that I had to be careful not to smear or tear. They were all dialogue with some visual descriptions, similar to how a play script reads. I had to imagine Donald and his nephews on these adventures since the story had not yet been illustrated. I wonder how many of those scriptwriters knew their story's fate (and paycheck) was partially being decided by a seven-year-old? The scripts I liked best were placed at the top of Father's pile that he'd read later but they'd already been judged by me, the audience for whom they were intended.

Sometimes I got to watch an illustrator take the story Father had given him and see the words now come out of Donald Duck's mouth. It wasn't the one-step process as I had imagined. First the illustrator began with a rough sketch and then traced or redrew the character adding more detail with each updated version. There were many revisions.

If my brothers and I came up with a comic book story ourselves, Father said he'd pay us $75 for a *Chip and Dale* and $150 for an *Uncle Scrooge* or *Donald Duck* story. There were many nights around our dining room table during which we tried to come up with ideas that would make a good story. One idea I had involved a dodo bird as the "Pride of Duckburg." In my story the Beagle Boys force Gyro Gearloose to make a potion that grows feathers on the otherwise featherless dodo bird. The Beagle Boys put the potion on all the birds except one that they keep to sell to the city for a large sum of money. But this dodo bird escapes and the whole city tries to recapture it for the big monetary reward. Uncle Scrooge wants to find it because he is greedy. Donald's nephews, Huey, Dewey and Louie, hope to find it because it is now a very rare bird and they believe in saving endangered species. The story's potential was limitless. Unfortunately, Father didn't have the time to help me shape the story into a formal manuscript submission format and it never earned me that $150.

Another time I suggested a story that began with Donald and his nephews talking by candlelight.

Father said, "You can't use candlelight."

"Why not?" I asked.

"The artists find it too difficult to draw," he explained.

I learned my first lesson. There were rules involved with writing, even comic books.

I'd go to lunch with Father at the Studio commissary. Father would point out actors, directors, and animators in the room. After lunch I always hoped Dad would be authorized to take me into the "Show Room." This room was full of merchandise from Disneyland. On rare occasions I'd be allowed in and sometimes allowed to pick something. I collected silver charms and there were some prized ones in there. My collection included Dumbo, Mickey Mouse, Donald Duck, Goofy, Peter Pan, and Dewey. These were exquisite in detail. I'd wear a different one on a chain to school depending on which character's mood I was in that day.

Other days Father would run errands. He'd take me with him to the Western Publishing's office in Los Angeles where Gold Key Comics and Little Golden Books were printed. Dad had written and co-written some of these. They were picture book versions of Disney movies: *The Magic of Mary Poppins, The Absent Minded Professor, Babes in Toyland,* and my favorite, *Supercar,* that begins, "10-9-8-7-6-5-4-3-2-1 Blast Off!"

Father had a soft spot for writers who might need a little freelance income to get through the month. Story ideas were bought and paid for by the number of pages submitted. He would encourage struggling writers to submit long manuscripts and paid them accordingly. One of these writers whom Father had a lot of respect for was Jerry Siegel, the co-creator of the superhero character Superman. Father often bought his scripts and then he and a colleague would edit the twenty-page script to the six pages required for a comic book story.

Father also worked closely with the comic book illustrators. As a consequence, we grew up knowing some of the great Disney artists. Carl Barks' drawings of Uncle Scrooge and Donald Duck were popular with the readers. Barks retired from the studio in 1966 to return to painting fine art. A client asked Barks if he could paint him a Disney character. Barks contacted Father to see if he could get permission from the studio to paint Disney's copyrighted characters. Father was able to get the "higher-ups" to agree. Barks' paintings were extremely popular. Approximately one hundred and twenty oils of Uncle Scrooge, Donald Duck, and the comic book covers were created. They became highly collectible.

One day Carl asked if Father would judge a beauty contest in his new hometown of San Jacinto, California. When Father said yes, Mother insisted on accompanying him. Father had a hard time choosing which of the girls to crown "Miss San Jacinto Valley" with Mother looking over his shoulder.

Because of Father's connection to the Disney Studios I enjoyed many opportunities that other children could only dream about. In first grade I had my picture published in the *T.V. Guide.* Disney arranged a photo shoot with Professor Wonderful, Julius Sumner Miller, who was going to be on the *Wonderful World of Disney* TV show. The Studio needed some children to marvel at his science. I could look amazed. Father sent us to the audition. Jim and I were chosen. In later years when I was in college this same Professor Wonderful did a presentation.

I went up to him afterwards and said, "I met you when I was six at Walt Disney Studios." I think he wondered how fast children grow up.

I always looked forward to Disney's annual Christmas party. It was quite the event and everyone dressed up. Mother would sew me a new dress, usually of red velvet with a white lace peter-pan collar. I had a warm long coat, and polished black patent leather Mary Jane shoes. Mother sewed my brothers' outfits as well. They wore matching red blazers with white shirts, short grey pants and skinny black ties. The event took place in one of the auditoriums on the Disney lot and there were other employees' children in similar attire. The Studio gave us more presents than we could personally carry. Santa Claus sat in an ornate red velvet chair. Each of us had an opportunity to sit on his lap and tell him what we truly wanted for Christmas. My wish was always a pony. Who better to play Santa Claus? Walt Disney himself. Santa Claus, Walt, did get a pony. After the film *Darby O'Gill and the Little People* was released in 1959, Ireland gave Walt two Connemara ponies. And all I was asking for was one!

Every Christmas party featured a screening of one of the latest Disney films. In 1964 it was *Mary Poppins*. There was a saying Father would repeat about how a wrong comment could "poison the well." The magic of *Mary Poppins* was poisoned for me when Father came home from the studio one day while they were filming and said the word on the lot was that Julie Andrews was a bitch. This was the first time I heard Father use such a word. We were told not to go to school repeating what Father had just said. When I watched the movie, I saw for myself how Mary Poppins could be rather harsh and standoffish.

After the movie, we greedily gobbled up the trays and trays of Christmas cookies provided. We'd head to the parking lot where Father's red convertible MG, complete with running boards, was left and would be our transportation for the short ride home.

Inevitably, Mother would sigh and say, "You children are definitely becoming spoiled with all the gifts that have been bestowed upon you."

My brothers and I loved the festivities, and the pile of presents.

Father came home from work one day and said, "We need to hold a family meeting."

Father started, "Walt met with me today about this idea he calls EPCOT, the Experimental Prototype Community of Tomorrow. He wants to create a planned community. It will be very progressive with public transportation, like the monorails they have at Disneyland. It will be designed in concentric circles with businesses at the core, schools in the mid-section, and houses on the outer edge. Walt owns some land in Florida where he plans to build it. He asked if our family would like to be part of the community."

I'd never been to Florida but I knew it had warm weather and ocean beaches. Going to school on a monorail sounded fun. I liked the idea.

Mother had the opposite opinion. She stated clearly she would not live in Florida nor be part of a "planned" city. Her answer was a definite "no."

Which is just as well since Walt never was able to realize this concept.

I belonged to the Mickey Mouse Club but not as an actress, only as a fan. I had the hat with the ears. I knew many Disney songs forward and backwards. I had a red and white record player that snapped together in a box with a handle. I played the Disney soundtracks from *Cinderella, Jungle Book, Song of the South, Snow White* and *Mary Poppins*. These lyrics would float through my head for days: "Just a spoon full of sugar helps the medicine go down," "Mister Bluebird's on my shoulder," "Wonderful feeling, Wonderful day," "Supercalifragilisticexpialidocious, even though the sound of it is something quite atrocious, if you say it loud enough you'll always sound precocious."

I could upstage my friends at school with the question and answer, "Can you say Supercalifragilisticexpialidocious backwards? I can: It is Dociousaliexpisticfragicalirupus."

Chapter 2

A Real Princess

I actually could have been a long-lost princess. My grandfather, Father's father, was Ransom Milsom Sherman. Family history, written in Swedish, has his ancestry going back to Harald the Fairhair, the first King of united Norway and Sweden in 860 AD. A separate lineage includes Charlemagne, born in 720 AD, and leads to Louis II, King of France 877-879 AD as well as Louis V, 967-987 AD, who was the last French King of the Carolingian Dynasty. Royal history continues three generations later with Baldwin V, in 1067 AD, who was Count of Flanders. His daughter, Matilda, married William the Conqueror in 1053 AD, sharing the English throne. Her lineage still produces the British Royalty on the throne today. This knowledge inspired me to read Swedish, European, and English history looking for the names of my early relatives. In the end, being of royal blood seemed to me to equate to one relative killing another relative for a chance at the crown. Maybe being a real long-lost princess really only secured an early death.

My mother, Nancy Fenno, grew up in the small town of Siloam Springs, Arkansas. She studied pre-med in college and headed west to obtain a lab technician certificate. Mom was attending the nursing academy in Pasadena when she and her roommate went on a double date with Father and his college friend Sam.

Mother had two brothers, Tommy and Johnny. Tommy was a wildcat oil rigger in Texas. Johnny stayed in his hometown farming and eventually bought a four-hundred-acre chicken and cattle ranch surrounded on three sides by Cherokee territory. Their mother, my grand-mother Eleanor, was born and raised in Siloam Springs. Her husband, my grandfather Buck, traded with the Cherokees and befriended them. He was invited to their sacred ceremonies and given many gifts including arrowheads and beaded leather. His collection was later donated to the Siloam Springs Museum. When Buck's mother needed assisted living, he built a nursing home he named "The Manor." Grandmother Eleanor ran this 100-bed facility until she sold it at the age of ninety-two. She was a self-made millionaire. Shortly after selling it she tripped on the rug at the post office where she'd kept the same post office box for ninety-two years and broke her hip. This injury created multiple health problems and eventually her death. For sixty years she'd visited the patients at her nursing home every day making sure they were being treated respectfully.

Both my grandmothers went to college or finishing school as it was called then. They were intelligent, dignified women. Helen White was the maiden name of my father's mother. She never liked her name. She said it was too common. When she went to college, her parents would send her a box of chocolates. There were so many other Helen Whites in the school that by the time the box reached her the other girls had eaten all her candy. Her grandfather had emigrated from Elgin, Scotland, to Chicago. He was a businessman in the right place at the right time and become vice president of Valvoline Oil.

Helen called once when she was moving to Florida and asked Mother, "Would you like the Steinway grand or Steinway baby grand piano?"

Mom decided on the grand. Jim was the brother who mastered its keys earning him the privilege of claiming it for life.

My father, George Ransom Sherman, was born in 1928 in Evanston, Illinois, the first child of Ransom and Helen Sherman. His only sister, Ann, was born four years later. His father, Ransom, was a popular radio comedian on a number of shows out of Chicago. Ransom's first job was as a "Song Starter." He was hired to attend banquets and when the meal was well underway, to stand and get the guests singing a dazzling round of "Yes Sir, That's My Baby." He found just standing up drew rounds of laughter and switched from singing (not his forte) to being a stand-up comedian. The best way to get paid for this occupation was live radio. Ransom was one of the original *Three Doctors* but when he held a cow-naming contest and pronounced "Flossie" was the perfect name for a cow, he was fired the following day because "Flossie" was the name of the radio sponsor's daughter. Ransom then teamed up with Garry Moore for the radio show *Club Matinee*. Daily Ransom would have to write a humorous script to be presented live that afternoon.

George would accompany Ransom to the sound studio and watch his father present his radio show. George loved the realm of live radio and spent hours building his own sound effects. He created miniature doors that could open with the right squeaks and close with a definite click of the handle. He built a pretend microphone stand and microphone with NBC painted on it. The wacky humor of Ransom's scripts would later serve Father well when he wrote his own "gags" for Disney comic books.

Ransom played different characters on other radio shows, including *Fibber McGee and Molly*. I have a photo of him from 1944 with Mel Blanc, Dorothy Lamour, and Bob Hope waiting for the live radio broadcast of *G.I. Journal* that aired for our troops fighting in World War II.

Ransom moved the family to Beverly Hills in the 1940s in order to work as a character actor in movies and attempt this new thing called television. He was in films with Gregory Peck (*Gentlemen's Agreement*, which won an Oscar); Cary Grant (*The Bachelor and the Bobby-Soxer*); and others. In 1950 he had his own television show called *The Ransom Sherman Show*. It was an ad-lib variety show with singers and skits and a moose head mounted on the wall that smoked cigars. The show won an Emmy, but the next day it was cancelled by its sponsors. He was a guest character on several TV shows, including *I Love Lucy* and *Father of the Bride*. At some point he just got tired of auditioning and left acting to work part-time for his brother, the magician, James Sherman.

A few years after retiring from show business Ransom found a way to travel around the world within his meager income. He booked himself as one of the few paying passengers on freighter ships. We would get postcards from places with exotic names: Bora Bora, Rarotonga, and Rangoon. One postcard came from Japan.

Ransom wrote: *"It was strange watching myself on television speaking Japanese."*

I could picture him in a bar in Tokyo looking up and recognizing one of the episodes of *Father of the Bride* and thinking: "*How did those words get in my mouth?*"

My father, George, spent his early childhood in Chicago. When Ransom moved the family to California, he transferred as a seventh grader to Hawthorne School in Beverly Hills. George soon became friends with Freeman Gosden, Jr. (whose father was Amos on the hit radio show *Amos 'n' Andy*). Dad would spend hours at the Gosdens' house asking Gosden, Sr. about the world of radio. Dad also loved music, especially jazz. Gosden, Jr., and he would go down to Crawford's Record Store and listen to the newest records. Since steel needles could damage a record, they were given cactus needles to use. One Christmas they were given front-row tickets to the matinee of a musical. The orchestra pit was directly in front of them. They both fell in love with the redhead playing the violin. They decided to write her a letter saying they were talent agents and would she be interested in auditioning for a play they were scouting for. Much to their surprise she wrote back, "Yes." That scared the heck out of them and they chickened out replying to her letter.

At Beverly Hills High School Dad was Senior Class President as well as a member of the school orchestra and band. He also formed his own jazz band that played for dances.

One evening Ransom came home and said, "George, get ready, we've just been invited to a music party at Jimmy and Tommy Dorsey's house."

Dad idolized the Dorseys. To him they were the quintessence of jazz dance musicians.

Father attended Pomona College where he was editor of the student newspaper, vice-president of his class and formed a new five-piece Dixieland band. As editor of the paper he'd dream up crazy concepts and with cohort Bruno Salmon. They would do photo essays such as "Sherman and Salmon go to Santa Anita Racetrack." There they did an article called "How to Win at the Track." Included in their piece was advice from Lou Costello, who said number nine in the third was a sure bet. They put their money on number three. Number nine paid $23.64 to win, their horse paid—nothing. While they were at the saddling stable they checked out the fillies both inside and outside the arena.

Their best advice was, "The only time to place a $100-dollar win bet, is when there is only one horse in the race."

Bruno and Father tried "their luck" at one other track. It was the Del Mar Race Track during fair season. They set up a penny-pitch con game. Everything was going well until the police showed up and gave them 30 minutes to get out of town—so much for becoming big entrepreneurs. Maybe it was this incident that later inspired Father to co-write a book with his Disney colleague Mary Carey titled *A Compendium of Bunk or How to Spot a Con Artist*.

On Veteran's Day the Pomona band was required to perform in formal attire. Very few musicians own formal attire much less want to wear it. Dad decided on a unique attire that was formal—in Scotland, kilts.

While at Pomona Dad became good friends with another student, Roy Disney, Jr. Roy told Father if he ever needed a job he should apply at his father's motion picture studio, Walt Disney Studios.

After college Father served two years, 1950-1952, as a Sergeant Major in the United States Army in Dachau, Germany. His job was scheduling bands to perform across Europe in hopes of lifting the spirits of post-World War II. He did have to pass a course for this job, "How to play the snare drum." He obtained military promotions for fundraisers he organized. These were Friday night poker games with all the proceeds going toward the entertainment fund. When he returned from military service, he married my mother in her hometown of Siloam Springs, Arkansas. He took up Roy Disney, Jr.'s offer and put in a resume at Walt Disney Studios.

Uncle Jamie was my grandfather Ransom's brother. He lived in a white column mansion in Beverly Hills. He'd made his millions by inventing magic tricks. This seemed a little dicey way to me to become a millionaire. What I hadn't realized was that magic tricks also meant "gag" tricks. A new "gag," such as the snake in a can, was bringing in $150,000 annually in 1925. Chicago in 1926 had seven magic shops within five blocks of each other. Jamie's was on the mezzanine level of the Palmer House Hotel. He owned the National Magic Company. Each magic shop had an owner who would teach their loyal clientele the secrets of a magic trick unique to their store. An ad in *Popular Mechanics* in 1926 read "Learn the Sherman Method." Gag tricks rose in popularity during the Great Depression.

We would visit Uncle Jamie in his mansion in Beverly Hills. Uncle Jamie married a woman we called Aunt Suzanne. She wore bright red fingernail polish that matched the red-flocked wallpaper in their living room. Jamie would show us his latest magic invention. If it was our birthday there was his "Magic Bag." We'd be asked to examine the velvet bag and at first inspection it was completely empty.

Jamie would wave a magic wand saying, "Abracadabra!"

We'd reach in a second time and there would be as many new one-dollar bills as our age. We would then be given a roll of nickels to use in the two slot machines he had in the basement.

He told us that the slot machines never lost yet; every visit we would try for three cherries and always came home empty handed. Also in this basement was a real theatre. There was a proscenium, curtains, and audience seating. This is where up-and-coming magicians could test their act in front of a live audience. Uncle Jamie had known Harry Houdini, Houdini's widow, and other magicians such as Harry Blackstone, Sr. and Harry Blackstone, Jr. Jamie would treat us to front-row seats for the annual *It's Magic* show. He'd also take us to Sunday brunches at the Magic Castle, another venue for budding magicians to hone their tricks. I seriously believed every child had a rich uncle with a magic money-bag. One much more generous than Uncle Scrooge.

§

CHAPTER 3

Overseas Comic Book Program

In the fall of 1962 Father was put in charge of the "Overseas Comic Book Program." From what I've learned this was an important expansion of comic book stories into the European, South American, Australian, and Asian markets. Writers in foreign countries were to bring out facets of existing Disney characters as well as create new characters to give the stories more variety and have characteristics relevant to their country. Tom Golberg was hired as Art Director to help manage the program. Overseeing the program was Father's boss, O.B. Johnston.

O.B. was a kind and gentle man who treated all his employees as extended family. He lived in a house in the hills above Hollywood. We'd be invited over for milkshakes. What we liked best was the hill in his backyard. O.B. would save cardboard boxes for us and we'd trudge up the slope and slide down in our boxes. His house was full of various treasures. One room held an extensive collection of oriental art with exotic swords and cloisonné vases. There was this amazing rubber plant growing through the roof of his living room. O.B. came from Ireland and to help his fellow countrymen immigrate he'd sponsor a young Irish woman to spend a year as his cook.

This often led to some funny cultural events. One Irish lass put an avocado in the oven and after 30 minutes she asked O.B., "How long does it take these to cook? This one is still not cooked in the middle," as she kept poking at the avocado's hard center pit with her knife.

After a year the Irish lass would be allowed to stay in America, and O.B. would sponsor her sister or cousin. He had a koi pond in front of his house, and in order to keep the raccoons from eating all his fish, he'd leave several loaves of bread out every night.

Father began travelling six months of the year to foreign countries to meet with publishers and attend book conventions. Each comic book story was given a code number preceded by a letter that identified the country or Disney department that created it. A "D" stood for Denmark, "I" for Italy, "W" for Western Publishing, the exclusive American comic book publisher at that time, and "S" stood for the Burbank Studio. Disney comics were being published in Italy, Denmark, France, Japan, Brazil, Argentina, Chile, Yugoslavia, and even Egypt (written in Egyptian Arabic).

Father's sense of humor went beyond the confines of a comic book. One colleague that travelled many times with Father was the London merchandising representative Peter Woods. He told me how he'd watched Father write poems on Hilton stationary, make them into paper airplanes, and fly them out his eleventh-floor hotel window to land at the feet of an unsuspecting pedestrian. Another time they were dining in a revolving restaurant called the Post Office Tower in London. Father decided to write a question, tape it to the window as it revolved past, and see if anyone responded. Someone did. Father then decided to see if they could raise some funds for charity by placing an envelope and note and asking for donations. They got some. I wondered what "charity" they "donated" them to.

Peter was in a hotel room one night with Father discussing what new comic book characters Disney should create. Superheroes were popular and they thought Disney could use one. Peter and Father came up with the concept for a superhero, using some magical device to give plain ole Goofy super powers. This was the birth of Super Goof. Back in Burbank Del Connell was given the assignment to further develop and write the first Super Goof stories and was credited with Super Goof's creation. Del has Goofy eating a super-powered peanut, called a goober, which magically turns him into Super Goof. Goofy can now can fly in his bright red long underwear (union suit), a blue cape and green hat. When the goober's power wears off, Goofy crashes back to the ground, and is his old self again, unless he has remembered to fill his hat with extra goobers.

I wondered if Peter and Father were in the pub too long or not long enough when they came up with this idea.

Peter said, "Your father took the future of Disney comic books very seriously and often was discussing plotlines, characters and how foreign writers could expand the Disney characters to reflect the humor of their country. Your father loved his work and would have done it for free."

Airplane travel wasn't as common in the 1960s as it is today because it was quite expensive. Disney employees were always flown First Class. Walt felt it was important to always project the image of Disney as a top-quality company. In First Class Father often sat next to a movie celebrity. He came home raving about what a delight it was chatting with singer Connie Francis on the ten-hour flight to London. I don't know how Mother felt, but I think I would have been jealous if my husband came home with such stories.

Father always travelled with an instrument, either his trombone or his saxophone. Although he wasn't performing in public very often he was constantly practicing and jamming with anyone who had an inclination. There were times the Studio had to book a second Hilton hotel room just for Father to practice his saxophone.

Before heading back to the United States Father would call home. If Mother reported that we were behaving well, then Father bought us gifts. Father brought my brothers a wooden castle. On other trips Father bought kings, knights and horsemen to equip the castle for battle. He brought me a doll from every country he visited. Some had a face carved from an almond or an apple. All were dressed in the costume of their country. I had dolls from Great Britain, including the Queen of England, a pair dancing from Yugoslavia, French dolls, many Japanese dolls, German, Italian, and Brazilian dolls. A few have disintegrated over the years, but most are intact. They were an inspiration to sew my own clothes and sparked my keen interest in different cultures.

When Father was not traveling, he was responsible for taking foreign representatives to Disneyland. He liked us to come along as little "emissaries." If there were any foreign representatives' children we were to be their special host.

The television show *Laugh-In* was big at the time and I vividly remember we had a great time teaching some Italian children to say "Sock it to me, sock it to me, sock it to me."

In my world, with three brothers, this meant if any one said these lines it was permission to hit that person. We'd then hit the Italian kids and certainly not tell Father.

There was another perk to hanging out with Father and the representatives at Disneyland. He had the Disney Gold Card that allowed all his guests to go to the front of any line, even my favorites "The Matterhorn" and "The Pirates of the Caribbean." I also loved the little cars that you drove on a track, but you had to be taller than the sign out front to drive one. I was jealous watching my brothers get to drive around until I was tall enough to join them.

If we didn't want to stay with Father we could wander Disneyland on our own with a Magic Key book of tickets for rides. We didn't know that other visitors had tickets that went from "E" for the best rides to "A" for lesser ones. Our tickets were good on any ride.

One skill I honed over the years visiting Disneyland was learning how to maneuver around awestruck visitors. I could anticipate the need for a quick right then double step to the left. I could analyze the situation quickly and find the fastest moving line. I never "cut" in line, but I could get to the front quicker than most. Sometimes when the rides had taken longer than anticipated, because we actually had to stand in line, I'd look at my watch and say, "Oh no, didn't Mother want us to meet her at Central Plaza thirty minutes ago?"

Fortunately, she loved to people watch.

We started to seek out areas where we could use our imagination and not just be part of the audience. "Tom Sawyer's Island" was one spot that allowed us to make up adventures as we crossed the rope bridge and climbed into the tree house.

There was another "ride" Disneyland had for a short amount of time called the "Forest of No Return." It was a room full of trees. We thought it was a maze to get through and proceeded forth.

"Wait, did that tree over there move? Jeffie, did you touch me?" I whispered.

Suddenly, all the trees were moving, crashing into us, grabbing at our shirts. Where were we to run? Once we'd escaped outside we realized we'd all been truly scared. The trees were all real people in costume with the intent of recreating the scene in the movie *Babes in Toyland* where the Forest of No Return attacks the children.

Father and Mother often asked us to meet them by "The Pirates of the Caribbean." There was a private club upstairs called Club 33 where they'd take representatives for food and refreshments. Mother loved their Monte Cristo sandwiches, ham and cheese, battered and fried. She'd pair this with a glass of chardonney. This was the only place at Disneyland that served alcohol, and it was not open to the public.

The ride "It's a Small World" opened in Disneyland in May 1966. Walt liked to bring authenticity, symbolism, and small details to his endeavors unknown to most. That year when Father was travelling overseas he was asked to obtain a vial of river water in each country. There were some countries he didn't travel to and we went to the Los Angeles airport to pick up a vial of water from Sweden. We then drove these all to Disneyland and parked in the back lot for employees. We went through the underground tunnel to the official opening celebration of "It's a Small World." Walt then poured these vials into the water on which the boats glided through. Inside the ride were dolls from many countries dressed in traditional costume and singing in their native language.

It's a world of laughter, A world of tears, It's a world of hopes, And a world of fears, There's so much that we share, That it's time we're aware, It's a small world after all.

When we were ready to leave Disneyland, we'd do a little shopping on Main Street. I liked watching the glass blower make swans and ponies. I'd buy some pencils and erasers for my school friends. Last would be a visit to the candy store. It was a hard choice between the large colorful lollipops or rock candy. I marveled at the beautiful crystals the sugar had formed. A sweet treat was bought to savor on the hour drive home.

One of Father's friends questioned him about why Disneyland was being built in the the middle of an orange grove and the geographical center of nowhere?

Father explained, "It was no ordinary amusement park. It would be kept very clean, and be a place of entertainment for children and parents equally. The company has done studies and Anaheim would someday be in the center of everywhere."

Walt got that one right.

§

Chapter 4

One Half Block from Walt Disney Studios

W̶e lived on a street called Parkside Drive, although the closest park was a mile away. The street one block west was Riverside Drive. It didn't have a river running along it but a freeway. Ours was a short street, maybe thirty houses total. The street ended at the back lot of Disney Studios. If we were lucky, or just imaginative, we could peek through the chain-link fence and bushes and actually glimpse *Follow Me Boys* being filmed. The other end of the street ended at Reese Place. This street went up a steep hill and was great for riding my pink Schwinn bike down, cutting the corner onto Parkside, and heading straight for our house at speeds that scared me.

Our house was in the middle of the block. The house was one story with tongue and groove siding painted white with black shutters for contrast. We knew most of our neighbors. Our side of the street had houses set back from the curb with large grass lawns. Some were 1950s ranch style like ours; others were Spanish stucco with those lovely curved windows and archways painted in earth tones. The other side of the street was sloped and the houses stood at the top. To knock on their doors to say "trick or treat" required climbing lots of stairs.

On one side of our driveway were bushes that grew little red berries. We weren't sure if we were allowed to eat them but we did. These bushes were wide and manicured into a neat and tidy rectangle that ran the length of the driveway. These were the perfect place for hide and seek. Another nice thing about our neighborhood was the drainage ditch in the middle of the street. If it rained really hard the center of the street would flood and we'd take out our beach rafts and raft down the culvert. It was a fairly flat street. There wasn't much danger as long as no cars drove through.

Our front yard was full of tall sycamores that were lovely to lie in the grass and look up at as their limbs and leaves swayed in the gentle breeze. They were a bit of a problem during our front yard flag football games because their limbs also blocked our passes. We called them "the great defensive players in the sky." We'd tear up old rags to wear as flags. I was good at both throwing and catching. I was glad I didn't have to tackle or be tackled. I wasn't fond of getting hurt.

In our backyard was a peach tree with a fort. We had an apricot tree and we loved apricots. The next-door neighbor also had an apricot tree with more apricots than we had. They were just too tempting and inevitably one of us would climb over the chain-link fence and find themselves up in the branches of our neighbor's tree.

Then the elderly neighbor would come out and say, "That is a mighty big squirrel in my tree today."

Our plum tree had the juiciest plums I've ever tasted, purple all the way to the core. The tree wasn't too tall but it still needed to be climbed to get to the ripe plums at the top. We always hoped the birds hadn't gotten there first. Jeff was up in the branches one day when he slipped and came tumbling down. The fall wouldn't have hurt much but his leg caught on a sharp limb and it was sliced open. Blood was gushing. Mother, having trained as a nurse, rushed out with towels and cord to slow down the bleeding. She quickly took him to the hospital. It took a lot of stitches to close that gap. It made the rest of us be a little more careful of the next tree we climbed.

I ended up in St. Joseph Hospital's emergency room three times. The first was when I was three. I stepped on the handle of a rake. The spiked end came up and put a hole, not a big hole, but enough of a hole in my head to require three stitches. When I was five I was at a neighbor's house playing on their teeter-totter. This was a homemade version with a long plank of wood bolted in the center to a hinge that allowed one side to go up in the air at a time. I was up in the air when I started to slide down the plank. I put my feet in front of me to slow myself down and ended up with a large splinter under my big toe nail. I would like to say I was brave, but I cried. It hurt, and again to the emergency room we drove. The third time was during a Sunday football game. A brother and I got tangled and ended up on the ground. I tried to stand but the ankle shot pain up my leg. I hobbled into the house and Mother took me to the hospital. There I waited next to a big high-school kid.

I was curious so I asked, "Why are you in the emergency room?"

He said, "I hurt my ankle playing football. Why are you here?"

I proudly said, "I hurt *my* ankle playing football, too!"

X-rays were taken and mine was only a sprain not a break. I never learned the diagnosis of my new friend.

Our dog, Freckles, was from the pound. She had soft short fur, brown and white patches of color, and a belly she loved to have scratched. I liked her floppy ears and easy temperament. She was a dog Santa Claus would want; round, soft and friendly. Father gave her a pedigree.

He called her a Scharpscher Spaniel. He'd tell our many foreign guests that she came from a long line of royal Scharpschers, a breed he had made up. We loved Father's sense of humor. He spent the day with ducks that could talk, so why not bring some of that imagination home into our lives as well. We were only surprised when the visitors believed him.

To fully appreciate this next piece is to imagine an old 35mm home movie in black and white with all the specks, and jerky motions. The game we were playing was "War" but there were no toy guns, grenades or other objects of destruction. The device we had was simple in concept and execution. It was a four-foot diameter tube made of cardboard that was three feet long. It was our tank. We could either walk inside it or make it roll by crawling. These tanks became our "bumper" cars. As long as the playing field wasn't fraught with stones or twigs the gliding was easy. With three others to attack, the strategies began.

Father had built a tall cinderblock cement wall in our backyard. It was primarily used as a backboard to practice tennis. It also had a basketball hoop and a large cement slab in front that was great for roller-skating. Dad called it the "executioner's wall." While practicing tennis, a ball often went over the wall and landed in our neighbor's backyard. They had stalls full of donkeys. To climb the fence to retrieve our balls was forbidden. Dad had once gotten too close to the back end of a burro on the Disney backlot and the kick he got left his thigh black and blue for a month.

George Davie was a writer who often visited around Christmastime. He lived in the desert and came bearing gifts such as dates, nuts and dried fruits. One year he brought a tumbleweed.

"Picked fresh this morning," he gleefully announced.

"This will make the perfect Christmas tree," Father countered.

The tumbleweed was secured to the living room ceiling and ornaments hung down nicely.

December also meant sending 350 Christmas cards to friends and Disney representatives all over the world. If my handwriting passed Mother's approval I was allowed to help address the envelopes. In return we got cards (and their stamps that my brother John collected) from every continent. One year we got a Christmas card from Salvador Dali. It was an etching of Santa Claus riding a reindeer. Dali was collaborating with the Studio on some special projects.

After Christmas, Mother asked, "What should I do with the tumbleweed?"

Father said, "Just put it out of sight behind the cement wall."

Blocked from the wind with lots of sunlight we soon had a tumbleweed forest. Again, not the easiest place to retrieve a tennis ball gone astray.

Our house came with a commercial refrigerator. It was large with a glass door. This was perfect for peering in to see what looked appealing: a slice of watermelon, the cherries that had just come into season, and the strawberries Mother said she was saving for dessert. I don't think she'd miss just one or two? In our garage was a large freezer. Besides meats and ice cream it often held boxes of Three Musketeer bars, Milky Way and Mars candy bars. Why we were given cases of these candies I don't know, but put a stick into the Three Musketeer bar and a frozen treat was created.

There was a narrow storage space in the hall entry. I can't speculate on what its intended use was. When my parents had visitors, I could easily slide in and listen to the adult conversation without being seen. Next to the living room was the playroom. It had a brick fireplace at the far end with gimbaled brass candleholders. Along another side was a large wood plank from an old movie set that was made into a bar.

I could picture John Wayne slamming down his empty shot glass and saying, "I'll have another." Who knows, this might have even been that bar from one of his movies.

Against the opposite wall was an upright piano and Dad's collection of instruments: A drum set, saxophone, trombone, kadiddlehopper, and basket of percussion instruments from around the world. I attempted to learn to play the piano. My teacher was an old lady who lived at the top of a steep hill I had to climb for my lessons. I wasn't gifted with Father's ear for music. He could play any instrument with or without sheet music. I couldn't keep a steady beat and quit after a few months. I envy those who can play by ear.

Father could play his instruments at work if time allowed. There was a room at the Studio that during lunch would fill with animators, writers and actors to play music in what I would call a jam session. Jazz was the usual style and many talented employees, including Father, dropped in just for fun. Eventually, a small group of animators (including Ward Kimball and Frank Thomas) formed a group to perform in public. They called themselves The Firehouse Five Plus Two and often played at Disneyland. Father had played in jazz bands, but this wasn't one of them. He had a fulltime job and four children at home to chase after.

Next to the piano was a Dutch door. The upper half could be opened leaving the lower half closed. It reminded me of the Emerald City Gatekeeper from the Frank Baum Oz books. This door led to our schoolhouse. Mother had found old wood desks with inkwells that were set in two rows with a chalkboard on the wall in front. We spent hours writing math equations on the board and challenging each other to solve them.

Father had a room called the den. It was off the formal dining room with a crystal chandelier. It contained a wall-to-wall bookcase, an old Royal typewriter, his India ink black fountain pen, and a window. The window looked out on the Japanese Garden he had designed and shouted at the cats and dog to stay out of. There was an oil painting of my Grandfather Ransom on the wall. It had been painted for his 1950s television show. Dad had a collection of pipes and tobacco. On one bookshelf was a signed baseball from his favorite team, the Chicago Cubs. On another shelf was a signed football from the Chicago Bears. On the other wall were two skinned snakes, a rattlesnake, and a boa constrictor. Up high on hooks was a cane. Dad took it down once and revealed it was really a sword disguised as a cane. The den was off limits to children.

There was an important house rule: If Dad was in the den writing—no noise. Right outside his window was the kumquat tree. This was the ammunition for many a battle. Kumquats are similar to tiny tangerines. The skin is eaten as well as the juicy interior sections. They are very bitter and we loved them. Our tree was loaded with fruit and their size was perfect for throwing at one another. This made for lots of attacks, running and yelling. It was three against one. My only option was to scream.

My two older brothers protected the younger one. I had to come up with a plan to keep from getting beat up. Hitting was included in "horsing around" and I didn't like being the target. I figured if I screamed before they hit me, then maybe, Mother would come out and stop them. Mother would come out and then send me to my room for distracting Father. Huh?

§

Chapter 5

Teacher's Pet

We walked the three miles to school every day even in the rain and snow. (I've since been told it only snowed once in Burbank in my childhood.) If it was raining hard Mother would drive to pick us up.

We always said, "We'd rather walk, there are lots of puddles."

It was then she'd hand us our rain boots and said, "Have fun."

I went to Abraham Lincoln Elementary School. It was a long rectangular building with a courtyard in the center where the kindergarten building stood safely enclosed. There were two playgrounds one at each end of the school. The right side yard was for the 1st-3rd graders. The yard on the left was larger with a baseball diamond and handball courts and it was for the 4th-6th graders. In the younger students playground was a ring-to-ring that I adored. It was like an umbrella without the fabric. On the end of each of the strands hung a chain with a solid metal ring attached. The goal was to swing holding one ring back and forth until I could grab the next one and go round and round the structure. I would race out of class at recess to be the first in line and there was always a line. I'd swing around and around until blood blisters appeared on my palms. From there I would go play foursquare.

When I began kindergarten, girls were required to wear dresses. Their length had to be below the knees. Thanks to the 1960s every year the hemline went up. I didn't have to buy new skirts throughout elementary school. We were privileged in 6th grade because Fridays were "pants day." Girls were allowed to wear pants. There were a few rules: No blue jeans—and they had to be long pants, no shorts. It was the one day of the week a girl could be a real tomboy. When joining the boys for baseball at recess, I could prove my stuff by sliding into second base.

For lunch we could order the hot cafeteria meal or bring a sack lunch. If we brought our lunch Mother would give us fifteen cents each. Five cents was to buy milk. The other ten cents could be used to buy ice cream for dessert or we could save it until after school. Then we would spend it at the hardware store on penny candy. Ten cents went a long way on penny candy. There were red licorice sticks to choose from as well as Jolly Ranchers, red hots, sweet and sour balls, Bazooka bubble gum, pixie sticks in numerous flavors that turned our tongues blue, Tootsie Rolls and sweet tarts. We could also wait until closer to home where there was a little market that sold a popsicle called the Big Stick. It was multiple colors and cost nine cents, which left us with a penny for candy. Sometimes I'd save up and for fifty cents I could buy a bright pink rabbit's foot that was on the wall behind the counter at the hardware store. These didn't last long. Our dog Freckles found them to be a favorite chew toy.

I was competitive at games at recess. I loved hopscotch. I had a favorite marker. Markers were important because they needed to land in the numerical order of the squares. I had to throw my marker into the exact next square. Rocks and pebbles tended to bounce. My marker slid into place. It was the key chain off the rabbit's foot from the hardware store. Another game I was good at was tetherball. I often won but found my arms the next day were black and blue with bruises from hitting and blocking that hard ball on the rope attached to the pole.

Young girls could choose to be either a Girl Scout or a Campfire Girl. My brothers were Boy Scouts (Cub Scouts at first) and I wanted to be a Girl Scout and earn more badges than they did. I was sick the day of the mandatory Brownie meeting for Girl Scouts in first grade. The only option left was signing up to be a Campfire Girl. Pre-Camp Fire Girls were Bluebirds and collected beads instead of badges. A Campfire Girl was required to sell boxes of candy once a year. I'm not good at asking people for money. I was sick the first week of "candy season." When I went to my neighbor's doors, they'd already committed to buy from another Campfire Girl. I was forced to set up a table at the local supermarket. I still had a cold and it was raining. I wore a scarf over my unwashed hair. I must have looked pretty pathetic because before I knew it I had sold my quota of candy. I discovered empathy was a great marketing tool.

I liked all my teachers except Mrs. Hopper in third grade. She had little patience and less of a sense of humor.

She would scream, "Don't slam the door."

This made her students compete to see who could slam the door the loudest. I was usually well behaved, but I was not about to let anyone tease or push me around. When an irritating classmate named Mark wouldn't stop teasing me, I finally reacted and punched him, not in the face, just on the shoulder. I had to stay after school and write, "I will not hit Mark, I will not hit Mark, I will not hit Mark" one hundred times on the blackboard. At the end of the school year I was dismissed early and on my last day I slammed that door as hard as I could.

It was in third grade I learned my first lesson about boy-girl crushes. I didn't have any but Frank had a crush on me. It was Valentine's Day and he gave me a box of See's candy. I didn't want his gift and gave it back. He insisted I take it. I asked a girlfriend if she wanted it.

She said, "Yes." There, problem solved.

Frank had been watching and took back his box of candy. Fine. After school he rode his bike to my house and told Mother how I gave away his present. Boy, was I in trouble. I was given a lecture on how to graciously accept gifts. It was not okay to give them away. I never ate that candy. Fortunately, Frank transferred to another school a few months later.

School came easy to me. My paper was the one the teacher used as a key to grade the others. My reward for finishing assignments early was to go into the hallway and play an autoharp. I didn't feel I was a very good singer but I could pretend I was on my way to Carnegie Hall when I strummed that autoharp.

I was usually the teacher's pet in school. Partially this was due to my intelligence. The other part was my ability to read a room. I knew when it was okay to be a smart aleck and when to hold my tongue and obey. Watching Father interact throughout the years had given me my earliest lessons about this—although Father hadn't quite perfected when to hold his tongue.

On one trip to Europe (we learned about this incident upon his return), he was crossing the border from France into Germany.

The German border official asked, "What is in your black case?"

Instead of responding like a normal human being and saying, "A saxophone," he said, "A machine gun."

This is *not* what you say even kiddingly to a German officer. Obviously, Father had not read this "room" right. He was quickly swept into the backroom and strip-searched. The German officers found nothing remotely humorous in Father's comment.

This was one time when Walt's saying, "Laughter is America's most important export," wasn't true.

Even though my classmates didn't always appreciate my teacher's pet status, I basked in it. Because I had teacher's approval I gained a self-confidence that allowed a little outside-the-box thinking while at the same time knowing when to play it straight. I think my grandfather's life in radio and movies gave me some insight as well as Father's ability to be a Disney executive one moment and dance with a Geisha dancer in Japan the next. I loved this juxtaposition of a corporate executive participating in another country's culture with dignity and joy.

Most of what I learned about being a leader in the classroom came down to plain respect. The same respect Father showed to the dozens of Disney representatives he met with regularly on his travels. If I could tune into the essence of a classroom situation I could add intelligence and logic, or take it to an easier plane of laughter and irony. Each method allowed for solutions.

§

Chapter 6

Play Clothes

After school one, two or three of my brothers escorted me on the walk to our house. Mother was always home when we arrived. It was required we change out of our school clothes into play clothes before we could go outside and begin a flag football game, often getting grass stains on the knees of our pants. If lots of the neighborhood children were out we'd switch games to kick-the-can. The bravest kids would hide in the bushes or climb the trees of our elderly neighbors. These neighbors didn't always appreciate us running across their well-trimmed lawns. On good days, however, they would offer us home-baked cookies and lemonade.

They would ask, "How was school? Do you have a girlfriend or boyfriend?"

The questions were a little embarrassing, but the cookies were delicious.

Our household had two Sunday traditions. First was that we had to participate in Sunday chores. Each child was expected to put in two hours cleaning house. My chore was dusting. I had to dust bookshelves, legs of chairs, the crystal chandelier, under the tables, every surface high and low. When one of my brothers became allergic to grass, mowing the lawn was a chore I took over. The second tradition was Sunday dinner. When Father was in town, this was a formal dinner. Children had to bathe and dress up. Ours was a family where etiquette was expected. Talking with food in your mouth, or elbows on the table, wasn't allowed. The meal was sophisticated. Father would often make a Caesar Salad, which involved cracking and mixing a raw egg into the romaine lettuce, tossing in olive oil, and fresh lemon. Last sardines were placed on top. I didn't mind the table manners, but I really didn't like being expected to eat sardines. Other nights Dad would surprise us. There was once a whole watermelon on a platter for dessert. Dad took the large butcher's knife, stood above the watermelon and dramatically said, "Kill!" while plunging the knife into the fruit, scattering juice all over Mother's white linen tablecloth.

After dinner we all headed to the living room. I'd grab my bed pillow, find a comfortable spot on the floor and wait for *The Wonderful World of Disney* to come on the television. If there were any stories Father knew about this week's presentation, he would interject them during the show. Some of the programs we watched Father later wrote into Disney children's books. *The Wonders of the Jungle* is one I remember him writing based on the nature films shot in the Amazon jungle. It was translated into eleven different languages. The book spurred my interest in ocelots as well as reinforced my fear of snakes such as the anaconda. Jim, John and I would egg Jeff to ask for a bowl of ice cream for dessert. He was my parents' favorite and if he got ice cream it meant we all got ice cream.

When I was seven, Dad taught us to play bridge. He made up a poster size "cheat sheet" that showed how many points each card was worth: Ace-4, King-3, Queen-2, Jack-1. It had the order of strengths of suits: Spades, hearts, diamonds, clubs. If my hand added up to thirteen points then I could bid my strongest suit. My brothers and I spent hours playing bridge. Dad taught us how to finesse, saving an ace and risking the jack in hopes of winning two tricks. Other concepts like ploy and gambit with subtle differences were explained and implemented.

These strategies were also put to good use when playing poker and gin. My grandfather Ransom was the supreme king of the card game gin. He would play it on a movie set with other actors while waiting for his parts in movies. They would play for money and he knew how to count cards. I don't think I ever beat Grandfather Ransom at gin but I learned probabilities and odds from him.

That same year I took a ballet and tap dancing class. I pictured myself a ballerina. There was a recital at the end of the sessions. Mother wasn't pleased at the required costume fees. Couldn't she sew my costume herself? I agreed with Mother. The costumes were expensive and we were not good enough dancers to need professional looking outfits. At the same time, sometimes if you dress the part, maybe in your mind, you become the part. I tested this theory out with my parents. I asked if Mom and Dad would like to watch me rehearse my dance.

They said, "We'd love to."

I bounded into our living room full of confidence that I am a serious and a professional ballerina. They both burst out laughing. They were in hysterics throughout my performance. I guess the costume didn't make a dancer. I didn't enroll in the second session of dance lessons.

Fortunately, I was pretty good at tennis. Dad was an excellent tennis player and great teacher. He volunteered on weekends offering tennis clinics to disadvantaged youth. He made up games within the game to enhance the learning process. He brought hula-hoops and if the student could return the serve into the hula-hoop they'd get a bottle of Coca-Cola. I wanted a Coke. I didn't get one. I wasn't a disadvantaged youth.

Mother did buy us a Coke a few weeks later. It was a hot day and we were at the lumber store. We asked Mother if she'd buy us a Coke out of the soda machine.

She said, "Yes, but you have to share."

It was my turn to have a sip and a brother thought I was taking too long and grabbed it from my mouth. Next stop—the dentist to see if he could do anything about my newly chipped front tooth. He couldn't. It would have been cheaper in the end if Mother had just bought each of us our own Coke (and I wouldn't have to live the rest of my life with a chipped tooth).

Being I was a tomboy I joined a girl's softball team. We were the "Sock-It-To-Ems." I played three positions: Pitcher, shortstop, and second base. Our practice field was an under-developed park on the other side of the freeway. The grass was bumpy. I was playing second base when I accidently put my foot into a ground hive of yellow jackets. With great fury they came tearing after me, just like in the comic stories Father wrote. I ran to the little creek in the park and sat in the water until they went away. Four yellow jackets stung me that day. I considered changing my position to catcher and I developed a fear of yellow jackets.

Mother cooked every meal from scratch except on election days. Our house was a polling place with four little booths set up by the front door and signs placed in the front yard that read "Vote Here." Mother would be too busy to cook. We'd have bakery doughnuts for breakfast and McDonalds' hamburgers for dinner. This was one of our favorite days of the year, although we did have to be very quiet while strangers tromped through our front door to vote.

Our babysitter lived right across the street. Her name was Sue and I worshipped her. Sue had a swimming pool. In my early childhood we didn't have one but she did and we loved swimming. The bravest sibling or the one who lost at drawing straws would walk those many stairs up to her front door and ask as innocently as possible, "Is the pool water very warm today?"

Mother taught us never to invite ourselves over to other people's houses, but we were allowed to drop hints. Some days it worked and we could go swimming.

Other days the answer was, "The water is too cold for swimming today."

Then the messenger would head back across the street with the good or bad news to convey to their fellow conspirators.

When Sue babysat we mostly played cards; hearts, poker or rummy. One rowdy night we asked if we could jump up and down on Mom and Dad's bed. Four of us were jumping at once. Then we heard a loud crack and the bed slanted left and downward. We'd broken a leg of the bed frame. Sue quickly thought up a solution. She felt five or six phonebooks would work to set the bed level again. Her father worked for Bell Telephone and she rushed home to collect extra phonebooks. That was a rare night when all four children were suddenly very sleepy and went to bed early. We wanted to guarantee we were deeply asleep before my parents came home and Sue had to explain.

I shared a bathroom with Mom and Dad that had a shower but no bathtub. I wasn't fond of showers.

When Mother insisted I needed one I'd say, "But, Mom, I went swimming today."

By the end of summer my normally blonde hair had a green sheen to it from the pool's chlorine.

There was a day I spotted the towel racks and thought what good pull-up bars they would make. They weren't pull-up bars and the towel rack soon bent.

The trouble came not that I broke the towel rack but when Mother asked if I knew how it had gotten bent I said, "No, no idea."

Breaking things wasn't punished in our house, but lying was. I was sent to my room until I happened to remember if I really did know something about the towel rack. It didn't take me long to confess.

I knew I was in trouble with Mother when she would call me by my full name: "Mary Catherine Sherman, you get in here right now."

The second give-away was when her voice would have an Arkansas twang to it. I recognized this accent from visiting her parents in Siloam Springs, Arkansas, most summers.

If I was in really serious trouble she'd say, "If your father was home he'd give you a spanking. Now go to your room."

I think she reserved this statement for when Dad was travelling. I only remember a few spankings in my childhood. Usually these were for trying out some of that new vocabulary I'd heard on the school playground. If the boys got caught saying these words at school, the teacher would wash their mouth out with soap.

For one of my birthdays Mother booked the party at a restaurant that included a fashion show. She enrolled me in one of the future shows. I was given outfits to wear, including a bathing suit. As I modeled the bathing suit past her table she whispered, "Pull in your stomach and stand up straight."

That was the beginning and end of any desire to model. From then on our birthday parties were held at home.

This was a time when Disney didn't release movies on VHS or DVD. This gave us the upper hand at birthday parties. Dad was allowed to check out a reel-to-reel of a Disney movie to take home for showing at our parties. *Jungle Book, Peter Pan*, and *Sword in the Stone* were my favorites. Neighborhood children would be invited into our playroom to watch the Disney movie otherwise only seen in theatres. Afterwards, ice cream and cake were served. I liked the little pink roses on the store-bought cakes. Last we'd play hide and seek with the whole neighborhood as our playground.

There were lots of rules in our house. You could never deposit or cash a birthday or Christmas check from a relative until the thank you note had been written and mailed. You had to wait patiently for a pause in an adult conversation to ask a question. You never shouted from one room to another but went within speaking distance of whom you wished to talk to. We were past the day of children are to be seen and not heard, but the timing of our contribution to the conversation was critical.

One outing Father liked was going to the Santa Anita Racetrack. Dad would take us out of school for a math lesson in probability. The interior of the racecourse was grassy with fountains and places children could run around between races. A blanket would be laid and a picnic set out. We all were to remember where "home" was. Then it was off to see the horses. Father strongly believed in reading the racing forum, getting a history of each horse on each type of track; wet, dry, muddy, and class of race. He had a few favorite jockeys. Always bet on Willie Shoemaker and if you know of any jockey having a birthday that was a sure bet as well. To see the jockeys mount their horses we would go through a tunnel under the track. Father did not like horses with eye blinders or their legs wrapped. I tended to bet on horses whose eyes and tails I liked. I was a conservative bettor and would choose a $2 show bet. This meant the horse could come in first, second or third, and I'd still win. These tickets didn't pay much but that was our lesson in probability and learning what a long shot meant. You risk more to make more. We all brought $10 of our own money and hoped we'd go home with a little more. $12 would be a good day. During each race one of us got to sit on Dad's shoulders. He was 6'2" and made a great seat to view the race. The rest of us would latch onto the fence near the finish line to feel the earth as these beautiful animals zoomed passed only a few feet away.

When driving home, there was often a cry from Father, "Heads down."

This was so he could see out the back of our station wagon.

If a car had come too close to ours he had these wonderful curses he'd make up and say, "May you get poison oak during your bachelor's party!"

It was a Saturday in spring when Mother said, "Dad just called from the Studio. It was snowing when he arrived at work. You should go look. "

We all dressed quickly and headed out the door for the long walk to the entrance of the Studio. It was only one block, but it was a very long block. When we arrived we asked the gatekeeper if he could tell us where the snow was. We also asked him to call Dad's office so we could go up and see him.

The guard said, "I haven't seen any snow and your father hasn't come into work today."

Confused and already tired we headed home.

Upon opening our front door Mother said, "April fools! Dad is still asleep in bed. Come in, and I'll make you pancakes."

When grandma and grandpa were in town I'd get kicked out of my bedroom (since it was easier to move one child than three brothers). I'd sleep on the sofa in the family room and have to "sneak" back into my room to grab some clothes for school. But we'd also get to go to my favorite restaurant for a special meal. It was called the Smoke House on Lakeside Drive. It was an old-fashioned steak house with red leather booths. Many movie stars and entertainment executives would hold meetings here. First we were allowed to order the drink called a Shirley Temple. This was a colorful beverage of ginger ale, orange juice with a splash of grenadine and a cherry on top. I insisted we order more than enough of the house garlic bread. It was sourdough toasted cheese bread. A neighbor, who was a waitress at the restaurant, smuggled the recipe to us. The crunchy topping was American cheese that came in a container similar to the dry parmesan cheese containers. I'd take the leftover bread home in a white take-out bag and "reheat" it over the floor heater vent in the living room. After a few days the bread would get hard and was a trick to bite into; nonetheless, it was my treasure from dinner out.

Mother taught me how to cook. Meringue kisses were my specialty. I needed to separate four egg whites from their egg yolks. The kisses used only the egg whites leaving the yolks for Mother to make into hollandaise sauce. Once the egg whites were in their own bowl, they needed to be whipped into stiff peaks. One cup of white sugar was added very slowly while still whipping to ensure the egg whites did not lose their stiffness. Last a teaspoon of real vanilla extract was folded in. Paper sacks were cut down to fit a cookie sheet and dollops of the egg white mixture were formed into Swiss Alps with a careful twist of the wrist for the curl on top. These trays were cooked slowly at 250 degrees for at least an hour. If cooked too fast it left the cookie's centers gooey. They could also be baked for the hour, the oven turned off, and left overnight. If cooked correctly they were crunchy, light, sweet, and had the ability to leave crumbs throughout the house.

Even though Father worked for Disney we still had to watch our pennies. We would go to the supermarket once a week and Mother had a strict budget we'd stick to. I'd take a push button adding machine and add up the cost of all the items in the cart as we shopped. If we were under budget we could grab a box of popsicles, if we were over budget we'd have to put back a package of store-bought cookies.

Food in the 1960s had its pluses and minuses. We were introduced to pizza, but when my parents ordered it, it always came with anchovies on top. On the other hand, the home deep fryer supplied us with wonderful treats. Mother made excellent onion rings, donuts, and French fries with the fryer. Her secret to great French fries was to cut the potatoes into quarter-inch strips, and then let them sit in ice water for an hour to get the starch out before tossing them into the hot oil. There was a cookie we made with what looked like a branding iron. These were called Swedish rosette cookies. The deep fryer had hot oil ready for the iron to be dipped into a pancake-like batter and fried. When cooled, they were dusted with powdered sugar, and placed in a cookie tin to be kept fresh and crunchy. We didn't have Jell-O at home, even though it was the rage across the country. Mother skipped that phase, probably because Julia Child's cookbook was her favorite. Mother's philosophy was if a recipe didn't call for butter and cream then it wasn't worth cooking. Mother could make excellent hollandaise or Bearnaise sauce to top our beef dishes. Hams were glazed with brown sugar and pineapple. There was always a dessert; fresh fruit and whipped cream, a vanilla cake with broiled or lemon-glazed icing. Sometimes for a snack we'd pick lemons from our tree in the front yard, slice them into wedges, dip them into sugar and quickly suck—the ultimate in sweet and sour.

Father would not eat salmon. He'd worked one summer in college at a salmon factory in Alaska and couldn't stomach it afterwards. When he was overseas, Mother would whip up dinners such as creamed salmon on biscuits. This was canned salmon added to a cream sauce and poured over Bisquick biscuits. Other "fast foods" were leftovers added to noodles, frozen peas, and Campbell's creamed chicken soup thrown into a casserole pan and baked for 30 minutes. Goulash was another reoccurring dish; ground beef, cooked, tossed with macaroni noodles and tomato sauce and simmered until thick. What delectable treats Father missed while he was abroad dining at five-star restaurants like his favorite in Paris, Le Mouton de Panurge.

Two blocks from our house, before the freeway, was a nice buffer strip of land with trees and grass called the polliwog pond where I'd go fly my kite. It was a paper kite with two-cross sticks, a rag for a tail, and lots of string. It was a Jolly Roger, black-and-white pirate design. I could fly that kite so high I could no longer see it. The challenge was reeling it back in before dusk. Sometimes the kite would get caught on the telephone wires that lined the freeway. On a few occasions it landed a bit west. West was the freeway. I could feel the crunch of the wood as an unsuspecting driver drove over it.

Sue, the family babysitter, had lived across the street but her parents bought the empty lot next door and custom built a new house. This time in the backyard they put in horse stables instead of a pool. These stables were just over the fence from our backyard and I liked going horseback riding. When I'd hear Sue out in the stables, I'd quick grab some carrots and stand on a box.

I would ask her over the fence, "Would Rusty like a carrot or two?"

This conversation would proceed to, "Are you taking her out riding today? Would you like some company?"

On occasion she'd say, "Yes."

I'd get to ride behind her to the kite-flying field two blocks away. There she would sometimes tie Rusty to a tree and let me sit on her. Rusty was not a fool and would walk closer and closer to the tree where low branches hung and that horse actually forced me off her back. Plop to the ground below. I thought that was one clever horse.

Our Thompson grape vine yielded a large quantity of grapes every summer. I ate all I could but there were many left over.

One year Father declared, "This year let's make wine."

We were to stomp the grapes, the old-fashioned way, barefoot. (One must remember, Dad is a comic book writer, he lived in a world of make believe.) I assumed a parent had read a book on making wine or at least a newspaper article. The grapes were left in barrels to ferment in our large cement basement. We went on our annual two-week beach vacation. Upon returning the house smelled—weird, potent, wrong. The "wine" had turned to vinegar. It took years for our basement to lose that odor. I think my parents needed to read the longer, revised edition of *How to Make Wine*.

Mother would wake up some summer mornings and declare it "Beach Weather." We were to gather our towels, rafts, fins, swimsuits, and flip-flops while she packed a picnic and gathered beach chairs. One of us would run around the corner and knock on the Donovans' door to see if our friends Annie or Patty wanted to join us. We'd all pile into our yellow station wagon and head to Santa Monica Beach. We'd park and trek the long distance over hot asphalt and sand to set up near the breaking waves. The children would spend the day in the ocean on rafts. The waves were not very big and it was easy to catch one after another. There was a pier a little further south that had an abandoned roller coaster on the end of it. Whenever I looked that direction, I felt shivers run down my spine; that ghost of a roller coaster creeped me out. After my long swim I would head to my towel. The only obstacle of the day was keeping sand out of my peanut butter and jelly sandwich. Last thing was the packing up and hot walk back to the car in my flip-flops for the salty drive home.

§

CHAPTER 7

The Jungle Book in Seven Languages

In May 1967 Father was asked to travel to Europe to promote a new animated movie about to be released, *The Jungle Book*. Father invited the family to join him on this six-week adventure. John was eleven years old, Jim was ten, I was eight, and Jeff was seven. We would leave in May and miss the last month of school. In exchange we had to do a report on one of the countries we would be visiting. My country was Italy. I liked that I could easily identify its boot shape and it had an interesting history. I couldn't imagine any culture allowing people to be fed to lions. I was excited about the opportunity to visit and see the Roman Colosseum for myself. My brother John did his report on Sweden. The Disney representative, Gunnar Mansson, had recently visited our house and John had talked to him about his home in Sweden and wanted to learn more.

Mother was a clever seamstress and sewed up calico skirts for me that were reversible. I'd get four outfits out of two skirts. I found out later I needed to carry lots of large safety pins with me. The minute a slight breeze came up my wrapped skirt would fly open. I had dark blue patent leather shoes with velvet ribbons, a matching blue velvet hat, and scores of little white socks. I packed a light blue raincoat and a few pairs of white tights that I was to be careful not to tear or get dirty. My hair was styled in a pixie cut—short and easy to comb. My three brothers had many matching outfits, red sweaters and grey slacks, items easy to spot in crowded areas. In my little purse I carried a lace handkerchief to cover my head in case we went into any of the historic cathedrals.

We flew into England and stayed a week at the Rubens Hotel, across the street from Buckingham Palace where Queen Elizabeth II resided. There was a doorman to open the hotel door and escort us to the desk, dining room, or elevators. London was easy to get around and everyone spoke English. There were numerous taxis and the Underground subway system to take us where we wanted to go such as the Victoria-Albert Museum. The exhibit on the history of fashion through the ages I found inspirational. I loved the fabrics, the textures, and detailed embroidery on these historical garments. It was a very large museum and my brothers, Jim and John, returned a second day by themselves to finish investigating the many fascinating exhibits.

We visited Father's colleague, Peter Woods, who was Disney's Director of Merchandise in England, and his wife Barbara. They lived outside of London in the town of Pettswood. We spent a day in their town exploring a park a few blocks from their house where during World War II tents were set up and filled with D-Day troops. A few miles away was the town of Bromley and the Biggin Hill Airport. It was here, during the war, where many pilots and airplanes flew in and out helping secure our victory over Hitler.

Father had given me a dozen charm bracelets from Disneyland: Sleeping Beauty, Snow White, and Cinderella. I was to hand them out as gifts.

In Pettswood I spent an afternoon playing with an English girl my age.

I said, "Wait here. I want to get you a surprise." When I came back, I handed her one of the bracelets.

She was thrilled. I thought I'd done the right thing. Later, Mother took me aside.

Mother explained, "Those bracelets are for other representatives' children. They are not to be given to just anyone."

I learned a sad lesson about corporate public relations.

One morning Mother suggested we walk around Buckingham Palace. She meant only us kids. We stopped to watch the changing of the guards. We tried to make a guard with his tall fur hat standing in a little box laugh or smile. He wouldn't. We walked and walked and walked. Finally, feeling lost, we stopped and asked a bobby where our hotel was.

He replied, "Follow the wrought iron fence around the palace and you'll get there."

We still had a very long distance to walk. We were very happy when we saw our friend the doorman.

The best part of England was ordering breakfast. We'd each get our own little teapot and teacup to pour our tea into. Just like playing make-believe but real. We took a day trip to Hampton Court and explored their gardens. They had a hedge maze that I laughed my way through playing hide-and-seek with my brothers at the same time trying not to get too lost because I knew my brothers wouldn't try to come find me if I did.

We visited many cathedrals on our travels. St. Paul's Cathedral in London was one of Father's favorites and I needed to bring out the lace handkerchief I carried to place on my head in proper respect for this magnificent church. I was always in awe when visiting old churches and cathedrals: Their beautiful domed ceilings, stained glass windows, and marble floors inspired my imagination to wonder what history had flowed in and out of their doors.

We were looking forward to visiting the toy store in London called Hamley's. Father had brought us many gifts from this store. It was seven stories tall and had all the trains, dolls, lead soldiers, and wooden castles a child could wish for.

We went to Madame Tussauds' Wax Museum on Baker Street. The realism of the historical figures made out of wax was impressive. I did make a mistake. My brothers taunted me to go with them into the basement exhibit called "The Chamber of Horrors." I already was plagued by vivid dreams of burglars outside my bedroom window at home, but now I saw what tortures would happen to me when I was finally kidnapped. Sometimes it wasn't worth the residuals of trying to be "one of the boys."

We took a ferry to the city of Amsterdam in the Netherlands. We stayed in a very narrow hotel. I'm not sure there was any other kind. Ours had a view of a canal. The children shared one room, and Mother and Father were on a floor above us. We took a tour of a diamond factory and visited museums. One day two Rolls-Royces pulled up in front of our hotel. My parents got in the first one, and we kids hopped in the second.

We got to say, "Follow that car!" to the chauffeur.

Another night a car, with a very kind Dutch woman, came for just the four of us. We were being taken to the skinniest restaurant in the world. It was three stories and six feet-by-four feet wide. I think its name was the Green Lantern. It was miniature, just like us.

One night in Holland a stranger broke into our room, while we were sleeping, and stole all the money our rich Uncle Jamie had given us—$100 each to buy ourselves presents. We think it was someone in the hotel who had overheard us talking. The next night I was too scared to go down the hall to use the toilet and none of my brothers would go with me. I wet the bed.

Our next stop was the Steiff Toy Company in Germany. They were making some characters from *The Jungle Book* movie and Father needed to give official Disney approval. These were stuffed animals: Baloo the Bear, King Louie, Kaa the Snake, and others. Steiff's stuffed animals have always been known for their high-quality materials often using mohair and their excellent craftsmanship. We were taken on a tour of the factory and the last room was a show room where we were told we could choose anything we wanted. I'd always liked the spiral drawing kits and choose that. As we were driving away, an employee came out to the car with his arms filled with Steiff stuffed animals which he poured into the car. A kitten puppet lives on my bedpost and Baloo on a shelf above my bed.

We travelled to some cities so Father could meet with Disney representatives. We visited others for sightseeing. There was the German Science Museum in Munich. It had as many floors as the toy store in London. We were thrilled to be allowed to touch the various scientific displays. We nicknamed it the "push the button" museum and spent hours enjoying all the fascinating exhibits.

There were also serious moments when a friend of Father's took us to the East Germany-West Germany border. It was an open field with barbed wire fences. On the East Germany side a soldier stood in a tall watchtower with a loaded gun ready to shoot if anyone tried to escape. We were told the field was full of land mines that would explode if you walk onto one. This friend of Father's *had* crossed this field to "the West" and survived. The thought of just a line, almost an imaginary line, separating families, haunted me for years.

There were lots of small villages we needed to get to so Dad rented a Volkswagen van. On a mountain road we made up the game of "zits." We assigned points for spotting objects; A pig was worth 10 points, a castle 25 points, and an old man with a long white beard 100 points. Then we saw one, the old man with the beard, and four children simultaneously started shouting "zits" at him.

There was a young girl at the side of the road holding a bouquet of wildflowers she'd picked. They were a collection of tall blue spindly cornflowers, white daisies, and big bright orange poppies. Father pulled over to ask if we could buy them from her. She didn't understand, got spooked and ran off into the nearby field. We hadn't intended to scare her.

Disney booked us top-notch accommodations. At night Mother and Father had representatives to meet for dinner and they'd sometimes leave us at the hotel. We were told we could order room service for dinner. We started a poker game and ran out of coins to bid with. We found that the top of the coke bottles worked perfectly for poker chips. When Mother and Father came home that night, there were far too many undrunk coke bottles opened merely for another poker chip. They gave us a lecture about only ordering food and drink you intend on consuming.

Dad spoke fluent German that was very helpful when we went on a tour of the Salt Mines. Father translated for us. The tour included riding on a small train/cart inside the mountain where the salt was being extracted. I imagined this might be similar to the type of place that Doc, Happy, Grumpy, Sneezy, Dopey, Sleepy and Bashful might have worked. The salt was loaded into carts, exactly like the one we sat in, hauled to the surface, and spread in warm places to dry.

Later, we took a boat tour down the Rhine where we got tired of counting castles. Castles lost some of their mystique for me that day. It seemed around every bend of the river was yet another castle.

We did get in trouble in Munich. My parents realized that if the children had a soccer ball to burn off extra energy, they could linger a little longer over their coffee. They'd tell us to find a café that sold ice cream, then play soccer until they were done with their breakfast and they'd come looking for us. This sounded like a good plan to us—ice cream for breakfast!

We found a huge green grass field and we were having a grand time kicking the ball back and forth when a man in a uniform belonging to the German police approached us shouting, "Stop. What are you doing? This is not allowed. This field was where Hitler gave many of his speeches and is a German monument, not a place for American children to be playing."

We'd never thought of a grass lawn as anything except a place to run around on.

The next day Dad was driving through the Black Forest when a lightning storm struck. Mom shouted, "All children to the floor."

If lightning struck the car, would laying on the floor of the car help? Eventually we stopped and got out feeling the van was too much of a target and we'd be safer by the roadside until the lightning storm passed over. Not much further along this journey, as Dad was driving, the steering wheel literally came off in his hands. He'd had enough. It was time to switch to trains. We were happy when we boarded our train to Italy and found "hamburgers" on the menu. We all ordered one only to be served ham slices. We were not sure where the "burger" came in at all.

We did learn where we could get a real hamburger. That was at the American Embassies' dining rooms. Included in the promotion of *The Jungle Book* was visiting American Embassies. Father would show a preview of the movie while we got real food. We saw *The Jungle Book* in seven different languages.

We took the train to Verona, Italy, and visited the well-known publisher Mondadori. It was his children we'd taught to say, "Sock it to me" on a car ride to Disneyland. We were given a tour of their printing facilities and then taken on an Italian shopping trip. Italy is known for its leather and Mother was told to choose a fine leather purse. I chose a white plastic purse in the latest style. My brothers were given a full-size foosball table that was shipped to our house in Burbank. We later donated it to the Burbank Community Youth Center. We were overwhelmed by the Italians' generosity but graciously accepted the gifts.

We travelled to Rome to see the Colosseum and Venice to ride in a gondola.

It was in Venice at the Piazza San Marco, covered with pigeons, that Father declared, "It is time for the 'Kick a Pigeon Poster Child' contest."

Father would photograph us trying to kick a pigeon. Finding a pigeon wasn't a problem. Kicking one was. We'd fed the pigeons at Trafalgar Square in London. Now I was in competition with my three brothers, Jim, Jeff and John. It only took a minute to put these two experiences together to get the edge on my brothers. Put food down for the pigeons to eat and then kick. Yes, I definitely got feathers that time.

We'd barely arrived in Switzerland when we begged Mother if we could rent a paddleboat and go out on the lake. Mom consented. There were only two paddles on the paddleboat, but eight legs wanting to paddle. We fought over whose turn it was again and again until Mother called us to shore and said that was not appropriate behavior. We lost our opportunity to paddleboat on a Swiss lake.

In Austria we saw lovely green hills that were perfect to roll down. We were quite good at amusing ourselves and proceeded.

For the second time we were met by a man in a uniform who shouted, "Stop. You cannot play on this grass."

We questioned, "Did Hitler speak here as well?"

Mother answered, "No. They are being silly to let such nice hills go to waste and not let children on them."

I wanted one of the Austrian dresses with red ribbons laced down the white embroidered bodice and a blue flouncy skirt.

Mother proposed, "We'll look for one in Salzburg where dresses will be cheaper."

When we got to Salzburg, the prices were the same and it was beyond Mother's budget. I did not get an Austrian dress and spent many years yearning for one.

In Innsbruck I got the pony I'd always wanted. It measured a half-inch tall and an inch long. It was made of pure silver and shaped liked it was rearing to go. I could hold it in my hand or attach it to a chain and wear it close to my heart. I collected little silver charms in every country we visited. I had a gondola from Italy, an Eiffel Tower from Paris, a little London bobby from England, and I was very fond of the blue windmill from Amsterdam that spun around.

Yugoslavia was on the coast with beautiful islands and friendly people. Father had to leave us in Zagreb for a few days and go to Istanbul and Romania, behind the "Iron Curtain," by himself. These countries were too dangerous for children. We'd been scheduled to go to Greece, but there was civil unrest happening at the time and we had to cancel that part of the trip.

Mother took us on a boat to the Island of Split. It was a beautiful and friendly island. I think a woman on the boat felt sorry for Mother having to deal with four children by herself. She invited us to her house for lunch. She lived was up a steep hill with beautiful views of the Adriatic sea below.

The hotel we stayed in Zagreb had the best dessert in the world. It was a hollowed out meringue filled with fresh strawberries and topped with whipped cream. My brother John bravely ordered the "Pheasant Under Glass" and from the back of the hotel we heard a loud squawk—John's dinner or just our imagination?

Father collected fine art when travelling, and at an exhibit in Belgrade, Mom allowed John, the oldest, to choose a painting. What he chose had a vivid color contrast: Orange and purple. I would call its style "Pop Art." It had a yin-yang quality that allowed it to be hung upside down and still read right side up.

In Paris we climbed the Eiffel Tower. There were lots of stairs. At the second level I had to decide if that was enough climbing or if I could make it to the top. I went to the top. There was a special Marc Chagall Exhibit at the Louvre Museum. We were familiar with some of Chagall's art because Father had brought home an original Chagall painting on a previous trip. These Chagalls were bright blues contrasted by reds and yellows. I loved the colors but didn't have a clue what the objects in the painting represented. We tired ourselves out looking at everything in the Louvre and were satiated by the numerous classical statues. At the Auguste Rodin Museum our favorite sculpture was "The Thinker." We later, back in the States, developed a dive into our swimming pool called "The Thinker" as we'd imitate the pose of the statue in our dive.

At the American Embassy in Paris I played with a girl from Australia. It was refreshing to speak English to someone my own age. For a whole afternoon we teased my brothers, hid from them, giggled and became instant friends. We exchanged addresses and were pen pals for many years. I was allowed to give her one of the Disneyland bracelets.

We'd visited many gorgeous museums. My favorite part was admiring the royal jewels and crowns that would be impossible to recreate today due to the forgotten craftsmanship and the cost of gold and precious jewels.

In our travels I learned how kind people could be to strangers. I discovered I didn't need "things" for entertainment. I mastered the ability to sit on a park bench and enjoy the smells, sounds and fresh breeze on my skin. I used my imagination to make up stories about the people that passed by. The trip was different from what I expected. It wasn't as much about doing or seeing famous sites but more about sitting, waiting for a train and appreciating the people walking by along with the smells and colors surrounding me.

§

CHAPTER 8

Summers Riding the Waves

Back in the United States we were fortunate that summers were summers. Mother didn't work and Dad could afford to rent a house at the beach for two weeks. For a few summers we owned a beach house in Newport Beach, California. It was a ten-minute walk to the ocean. We'd pass the Frog Shop where we would buy strong navy-blue canvas rafts. These were a roller coaster in an inflatable package.

Wearing a t-shirt over my bathing suit because the raft would rub my skin raw as I paddled, I could conquer the highest swell I was brave enough to attempt. The ocean was a natural amusement park filled with rides more thrilling than any run on electricity. Here I was, not more than 4 feet tall, with only air between the white water and myself. There was a gradation of waves to choose from. The swells closer to shore were 1-2 feet tall and gave a short gentle ride. There were sets of middle-size waves 3-4 feet that were safe with some thrill. I'd be positioned on top of the swell, with fast paddling, I would swoop down the front of the wave. I'd try to keep my balance so I wouldn't tip over and end up in the white foam with sand filling my bathing suit. The best, most challenging waves, were the outside sets that came every 20 minutes. It took some strength and paddling to get over the middle swells without being accidently caught and pulled back to the beach. Once past these I'd have a few moments of rest and calm while waiting to see where the large set would emerge. Sometimes I found myself in over my head. The waves were larger than I had anticipated. If a wave was about to break in front of me, I had no choice but to abandon the raft and dive to the ocean floor beneath the undertow until the impact of the ocean current washed over. With all my strength I'd kick off the ocean floor to reach air and hope another wave wasn't waiting right there to trounce me. Sometimes I missed my timing and went rolling and rolling with the white water as it carried me to shore. I'd be left a little out of breath, embarrassed, and happy to be on solid ground. There was a day while waiting for an outside set I found myself in the right place at the right time, exactly where the swell was peaking. At the crest of this wave I looked down thinking *what the heck have I done? This is at least an 8-foot drop!* Whether it was or not, it was in my mind. I considered back paddling, but it was too late, the momentum of the wave had me, going over the falls was my only option. I held tightly onto my raft, screamed, and found myself heading for the biggest thrill of my life. I did it. I survived the wave. I didn't fall off and I rode that wave all the way to shore where I got the sand out of my bathing suit and took my victory to my towel.

Our beach house neighborhood sponsored a clubhouse. It had a pool with a swim team, a daily crafts activity and a snack area. I joined the swim team. We swam against other neighborhood clubhouses. One week we were going to compete against a team that didn't have a swimming pool but sectioned off part of the bay as their swimming area. Swimming in a bay made me anxious. I'd been warned, whenever in a bay, not to let my feet touch the ground because I could step on a sting ray and their tails would swing around and sting me in the back of my heel. Our coach wanted us to practice in the saltwater canal next to our clubhouse for this meet. I didn't want to. I did, though. Coach was standing by with popsicles for everyone. On the day of the meet I did my best to tread water until my event was called. I don't remember how I placed. I do know over the summer I collected blue, red, white and pink ribbons. Our swim team came in first place. But, I still have a fear of swimming in estuaries and bays.

The fragrance surrounding our beach house was delicious. The garden was full of jasmine bushes that sweetened the air all summer. There wasn't much of a yard, but the warm beach air and smells made it feel immense.

The house had a sliding glass door leading outside. In my excitement to get to the pool, I walked right into it. Shards of glass landed everywhere, including my knee. One would think that doing this once I would have learned my lesson. No. A few weeks later I walked into the new sliding glass door, again sending glass flying. It was a good thing my mother had studied to be a nurse and was excellent with a pair of tweezers. I might have hoped I had the power to walk through walls, but I didn't.

Dad would travel the hour to the beach house on weekends. The first Saturday he came he needed to bring our Siamese cat Corey with him. Cats aren't fond of car travel or new territory and Dad didn't help. He was driving his TR3 convertible and decided the best place for the cat was locked in the trunk. Needless to say, that when they arrived and Dad opened the trunk the cat jumped 6 to 8 feet in the air and took off. We didn't see her again for two weeks. When she was finally brave enough to return, she looked mangy and was very hungry. We were very relieved she came back.

There was one activity at the beach I participated in but didn't savor the results. This was clamming. At very low tide we would spread out on the beach and dig into the sand with the heels of our feet. If we hit a hard object it was a clam. We collected these in a bucket. Once we gathered enough we'd walk the four blocks back to our beach house where Mother either put them in a pot of boiling water or in a mesh fireplace prong that would smoke them. The clams would open when cooked. Mother loved this for dinner. I had a problem eating a living thing I'd seen killed. There was often sand still mixed in with the mollusk. I vehemently refused to eat them. Other times we'd walk to the pier and bring home a bag of live crabs, their pinchers still active. Again, Mom would throw them into the pot of boiling water. I couldn't bear to eat the crab either. Good thing I liked peanut butter.

After one summer, we sold the beach house, and built a swimming pool in our backyard. It had a diving board that we spent hours on, making up dives. We even invented a game. It was pool baseball with a plastic bat and ball. The batter would stand in the shallow end. The pitcher would throw the ball from mid-pool. What we hadn't thought about was that gradually the light plastic ball was filling with water and becoming heavier. One pitch was thrown a little too fast and right into the leaded glass window behind the pool. Leaded glass windows are expensive. We were ordered to retire that game.

Another favorite game was dibble dabble. One of us dove to the pool's bottom with a toothpick while the others turned their backs. When a player saw the toothpick, they called "dibble dabble" and jumped in to retrieve it. If they missed, the others had a chance to try for it. Mother wondered how I could see a toothpick in the water without my glasses. I am not sure how, but I could.

There was the day I was really not thinking. We had the beach rafts in the pool to float around on. I thought it would be interesting to see if our Siamese cat wanted to float around, too. What I forgot was that cats don't like water and their first instinct is 20 claws extended—puncturing the raft I'd tossed her on.

§

CHAPTER 9

A Typical American Family

Father was in charge of Foreign Relations at Disney Studios. This meant our house was often the destination for foreign guests to experience "a typical American family." Mother was an excellent cook and could give the Disney Representatives an American dining experience complete with four mostly well-behaved children. One evening representatives from three different countries ended up at our house for a dinner party. The women all wanted to cook a specialty from their country and Mother became kitchen manager. She needed to make sure these women had the ingredients they needed as well as bowls, pots and pans. There were three women sharing our small kitchen and none spoke English.

The Italian Senora was cooking her favorite Italian pasta. We apparently didn't have the right size pots and pans. She'd use her hands to describe to Mother what she wanted and Mother would send us to our neighbors to borrow what we hoped she needed. Every time we'd enter the kitchen with our newly acquired findings Senora would shake her head "No, no, no." Off we'd go again never really sure what we were looking for but accepting whatever any neighbor was willing to loan us. I think we hit every house on our street before Senora was satisfied.

One of the other women in the kitchen was Japanese and she was cooking what to this day I consider the best chicken I've ever tasted. She marinated chicken wings in some variation of teriyaki sauce and fried them in a way that made them tender and mouth watering. The third cook was from Argentina and decided the barbecue out back would work for her meal. She made some lovely barbecued beef with just the right balance of herbs and lemon. It was a colorful, chaotic and eventful night.

Father often organized a card game in the playroom when foreign representatives were visiting. He set up a large round table and the men sat around with bourbon and cigars and proceeded to play the international game of poker. Someone was needed to convert the different currencies into a common one. Dad put me in charge of selling poker chips. I was very fluent in math. I got to sit at the grown-up table all night as banker. The games would go well past midnight and Father said to sleep in even though it was a school day. When I would wake up at noon, he sent me to school with a note for my teacher, "Please excuse, Cathy was up late playing poker. George." My brother John's tardy excuse read, "Please excuse John not doing his homework, he had to stay up late learning about the odds of an inside straight." My school loved Dad's sense of humor and there had no problem excusing our tardies.

Another evening some Japanese representatives were invited to our house for dinner. One couple came bearing gifts. The wife had brought me a complete kimono outfit. The outer kimono was a bright red textured silk with yellow flowers. There was a pink silk slip that went under it. She gave me some funny white socks with a slit in the toes in order to be able to wear the platform shoes called zoris. These had a thong between the big toe and little toes. She brought soft silk belts to wrap the kimono and keep it closed. There was one large stiff heavy belt called an obi with a bow in the back to complete the outfit. She also had hairpieces, little embroidered balls, for dangling from hair pilled into a bun. The kimono was six inches too long. This very patient woman asked for a needle and thread and spent an hour hemming the under slip and outer kimono so it fit perfectly. I was impressed by such a generous gift and a little embarrassed having to model it in front of the other representatives. It was too precious a gift to ever give away and still hangs beautifully in my closet.

Around 1968 Father wrote and edited a magazine called *The Wonderful World of Disney*. It was distributed for free at Gulf Gas Stations. Father enjoyed putting it together. He had free reign to set up interviews with people he respected such as astronaut Michael Collins or the baseball player Ted Sizemore, Los Angeles Dodgers Rookie of the Year. The magazine included articles on nature, a behind-the-scenes look at Disneyland, and comic book stories featuring Fethry Duck. There were mazes and crossword puzzles, "How to Draw Mickey Mouse," and "Goofy Learns to Surf," an article my brother Jim wrote and was paid for. There were articles on American History and National Parks. Each edition had a poster of the "Monster of the Month." My favorite was Madam Mim in her dragon transformation. She reminded me of the Peter, Paul, and Mary song, "Puff the Magic Dragon," that I'd learned at school. George Davie rewrote some classic fairy tales such as "Little Red Riding Hood," giving them a modern approach. He also came up with some rather silly morals: "Some grandmothers deserve to be eaten up by wolves." I wrote a poem that was published in the first edition. The limerick read: "There was an old man with a mule. He taught him to swim in a pool. The first time he tried, he drowned and died, and that was the end of the mule boo hoo." Maybe not great literature but it went out to thousands of people. Again, as competitive children, we fought over who got the magazine first and then would do the mazes and puzzles before a brother had a chance. I'd also give Father feedback.

"Dad, this 'Find Things with the Letter 'B'' is all wrong. There isn't a Beanie or Belt but there is a Bluebird and a Bush."

Father replied, "Then write 'A Letter to the Editor' telling them of their mistakes."

I did and that got published. If only they'd run those picture puzzles by me first those mistakes would never have gotten to print.

We inherited a trunk full of magic tricks from Uncle Jamie's estate. In this trunk were dozens of silk scarves that had once been up a magician's sleeve. There was a "Where is the Ball?" set. We could practice switching the little foam ball under three large thimble-shaped metal glasses, turned upside down, until the "mark" was confused and would not be able to identify which glass held the ball. What looked like a Bundt cake pan had a false bottom where a dove would be place until "Abracadabra" and out would fly the bird from the cake. We never quite got the hang of that trick because we didn't have a dove to practice with. My favorite trick in the trunk was the finger guillotine. The magician would place a carrot into the hole, and with some dramatics, a drum roll please, the guillotine would fall, and the carrot would be sliced in two. Next we needed a volunteer to put their finger in the hole. *What no volunteers? How about you with the yellow shirt? Yes, you. Come right on up. It is a simple matter of putting your finger through here and clinking your heels three times "there is no place like home, there is no place like home, there is no place like"* . . . and the blade would fall. Miraculously, this time, the finger would exit still attached.

Since Mother sewed, Halloween meant choosing a fantasy and watching her create it. One year all four of us were "Jack-in-the-boxes." We wore clown costumes and a decorated cardboard box. We would sit inside the box and suddenly pop out in our costume.

Every year at school we would march in a circle in front of a line of judges who'd choose which student would win Best Costume. I thought I had it the year we'd returned from Europe. I had real wooden shoes from Holland. Mother sewed a Dutch costume to match. I walked in the judging circle hoping they would pick me. They didn't. Just for the record, wooden shoes are hard to walk in.

The next year I was in love with a picture of a dress in a children's book. It was Marie Antoinette style and had an overskirt that gathered up in little scallops with a little pink bow to accent the curves. Mother sewed it using the picture in the book as her guide. She chose a soft pink satin fabric with a pink chiffon overskirt. I wore the dress on Halloween to the school costume parade equipped with a crook. I was "Little Bo Peep." I spent the day looking for my lost sheep (I never did find them). But, I did win the prize for Best Halloween Costume and I was thrilled.

Living close to Hollywood we often went to theatrical productions. We saw Mary Martin in *Peter Pan* and Yul Brynner in *The King and I*. The first book I read from the adult section of our public library when I was nine years old was *Anna and the King of Siam*. I was very fond of the story on which the musical was based. The title of a play I liked best was *Don't Bother Me, I Can't Cope*, a musical celebrating the American-African experience. Before the performance began I was allowed to go up to the front of the theatre to the orchestra pit and watch the musicians tune their instruments. It was this combined artistry that I found inspiring: The musicians listening to the actors' cues and the actors' listening to the musicians' cues.

What really matters to children growing up? In my experience, it is having a parent with an endless supply of cookies, homemade popsicles, and a tolerance for rough housing. Allowing children to stay up late reading, and if they are still hungry having a mother who will bring them a cut-up apple in bed. A parent's true interest when asking, "What happened at school today?" Or "Do you need help with your homework?" All right, that last statement wasn't always true. Father was an editor. An editor who didn't believe any writing whether a piece of fiction, report or essay should be submitted until seven versions had been written, edited and revised. He had a black India ink fountain pen engraved with his name that he would take out to correct my grammar and underline words I was to look up and check if they were spelled correctly. He told my fifth-grade teacher not to give me an "A" in spelling because I couldn't spell. Yet, spelling tests were about memorizing the words and their spellings so I could get "A's." Spell check hadn't been invented. My teacher gave me a "B" in spelling that term in response to Father's speech. I didn't think this was fair. Would Goofy or Donald have put up with this?

Fridays in elementary school were folk dancing day. I enjoyed learning the steps, sashaying, the laughter when we messed up and the semi-flirting that occurred. The boys, on the other hand, weren't thrilled. Maybe because they thought it was "sissy," or girls still had "cooties" or maybe it was just "cool" to protest. One particular boy, Tom K., in our class liked to hand out raw garlic to the other boys to chew right before the record player started going. Needless to say, it wasn't unusual for the girls to prefer to dance with other girls who at least had fun and would giggle.

Mr. Roosman was my fifth-grade teacher. I liked that he played the guitar. He'd teach us songs by Peter, Paul and Mary, Bob Dylan and Woody Guthrie. He'd explain why these songs were written and the history behind them. "Blowin' in the Wind," "This Land is Your Land," "500 Miles," and "If I Had A Hammer" were songs about the poor man's struggles: Coal miners who'd set up credit at the company store only to be forever in debt; the cost of war in human lives; the immigration to the West where trees were said to be full of fruit waiting to be eaten. Mr. Roosman brought the culture of the 1960s into the classroom and explained it to his students through the creative use of song lyrics.

I asked Dad to write me a play to perform in this class. I said I wanted it to have a Prince, a Princess, a Dragon and a Flower. Dad titled the play *Going to Pot*. He named the flower Mary Wanna. I had wanted to be the Princess but after reading the script I decided it would be much more fun to play the Flower. The Prince and Princess pick the leaves of the "flower" daily for the Dragon to light up for them to smoke. We were actually allowed to present this play in class. I liked Dad's costume descriptions: "The Prince is dressed as much as possible like the Jack of Hearts, failing this, the Jack of Diamonds, only without a bath. The Princess is dressed in a shroud embroidered with a Scarlet Letter on the back, any letter." And Dad thought the 1960s were censorious times.

Fifth-grade students were allowed to opt for a class in learning to play an instrument. I had the cutest instrument available to me, a soprano saxophone. I pictured myself standing beside Father on his alto saxophone and me with an instrument just my size playing as well as he did.

The music teacher said, "I can't teach you the soprano saxophone. There is no music written for it."

I didn't understand. I thought if I had a playable instrument then there was a spot for me in the band.

He said, "I'll teach you the clarinet, but I can't teach you that saxophone."

I was very discouraged and never did learn to play an instrument.

Sixth graders were required to put on a school play. The teachers would write the script and the students would do the rest. Our graduation play was about a schoolteacher who takes her class on a field trip to Mexico. I really wanted to be the one who switched the lights on and off. If not that, then the one who got to open and close the curtain, but no, I was given the lead role—the schoolteacher. Now, this play had Spanish words in it. I have pronunciation issues with English words. I can still feel my face turning red as I stumbled over words like: Chichen Itza, Teotihuacan, Tenochtitlan and Cuicuilco. Maybe this was the real beginning of my stage fright and the inspiration to graduate college with a degree in *backstage* theatre.

As a final departure, Abraham Lincoln Elementary held a graduation dance. To make sure every sixth grader got a chance to participate we were given dance cards to be filled out a week before the event. I felt I'd made a coup when I got Garry to sign on the last dance, a waltz. I'd had a crush on him for three years and since we were moving that summer to a different town I wanted to tell him and give him a goodbye kiss. The school had asked Father to be the Master of Ceremonies. The night went well. No one spilled punch on my dress.

When we came to the last dance, Father announced, "Throw away those dance cards, choose any partner and we'll replay your favorite song of the night."

I didn't get my slow waltz with Garry. For years I was a little steamed that Father accidently blew my first romantic plans and made the old adage, "Sweet sixteen and never been kissed," a reality.

§

CHAPTER 10

How Mary Poppins Almost Got Father Killed

Father travelled all over the world to meet with Disney representatives and attend Disney Conventions and International Book Fairs. Mother was invited on some of the European business trips and Grandmother Eleanor would come stay with us for the two-three weeks they were gone. Disney's International Conventions were held in various cities around the world. Walt and Roy would attend as well. Approximately twenty countries' representatives would be present for the week's events.

Over seventy representatives were in attendance at the 1959 Fifth Annual Disney Convention. Most representatives stayed at the Dorchester Hotel on Park Lane. These annual meetings were important to make sure all the Disney representatives knew exactly what direction Walt and Roy envisioned the future of Walt Disney Studios. Reports from each country's chief executives were presented. New publishing ideas as well as merchandising strategies were discussed. Every morning and evening there were screenings of Disney's latest movies released or about to be released. Quoted from the brochure: "All work and no play has a dulling effect on the intellect, so Wednesday night will be an evening out to the theatre." There were four choices of theatrical productions with already reserved seats to choose from.

For the wives at the London 1959 conference their schedule started with lunch at the Savoy and an afternoon Daimler coach sight-seeing tour of London sights. The next day a special fashion display held at Hartnell's, the Queen's dressmaker, was arranged. The third day the wives were invited on a tour of the House of Commons hosted by Mr. George Oliver, M.P., with lunch in the House of Parliament. The next two days were trips to Oxford and Stratford-on-Avon as well as another fashion show at Worths on Grosvenor Street.

Father's colleague Wendall Mohler was attending his first Disney Convention in 1965 and they were flying with their boss O.B. Johnston. Wendall wasn't sure how to fill out the British entry form. He didn't know if he should state his visit as tourist or business. He asked Father what he was claiming. Father showed him his form and in bold letters Father had written "MASTER SPY." Wendall thought this was pretty funny and put down "Demolition Expert." By the time they landed and were approaching customs Wendall was a little nervous and having second thoughts. When they got to the counter, the Custom Agent looked them up and down a few times before passing them through. If you traveled with Father you had to be up for a sense of adventure.

Later in spring they were headed to Mexico City, Bogota, Colombia, and Caracas, Venezuela. A meeting of all of the South American film and merchandise representatives was taking place in Caracas. The Academy Awards were also being held in Hollywood and the movie *Mary Poppins* was up for thirteen Oscars. Card Walker, President of Disney, was anxious to get the Oscar results; however, Caracas is five hours ahead of Los Angeles. Father and Wendall, along with Elcan Disendruck and Maurice Silverstein, the Brazilian and Venezuelan representatives respectively, went to the newspaper office to wait for the results. It was close to 2:00 a.m. when they learned Julie Andrews had won Best Actress for her role as Mary Poppins.

There was political unrest in Venezuela at the time. An ex-dictator had been jailed, and there were armed militia roaming the streets looking for weapons, suspicious people, and simply robbing and killing. The four Disney executives got into a taxi to take them back to the hotel. Just before crossing a bridge uniformed soldiers surrounded their cab and demanded they stop. They were told to step out of the cab, at which time guns were pointed at their heads.

The Venezuela representative quickly explained, "We work for Walt Disney . . . Mickey Mouse, Donald Duck, Disneyland . . . ."

One of soldiers must have been a fan because they were immediately released.

When Father was travelling, he formed a game he'd play with his colleagues. It was similar to the "Zits" game we played. He had a point system with rules he made up as he went along. One day it might be: 10 points for a good looking blonde with brown eyes; 20 points for a redhead carrying flowers; and 30 points for a brunette wearing a fur coat. While eating or sightseeing they'd keep track of who saw her first and at the end of the day a prize, which Father had brought from America, would be given to the person with the most points.

Once a year O.B. Johnston would fly all of the foreign representatives to the Disney Studios in Burbank for an annual meeting. For the Disney Annual Convention at the Studios in 1965 Father decided it was time to "break" the traditional dress rules and wear a turtleneck instead of shirt and tie with his dress jacket to the event. He convinced his colleague Wendall to follow "suit" in support. Father, similar to myself, enjoyed trying to get away with something slightly outside the rules. The only person who said something was Roy Disney, Senior.

Roy said, "Looks good." Father had gotten away with it again.

O.B. Johnston would do his best to make everyone feel welcome and part of an extended family. Walt, on the other hand, was more of a taskmaster with very strict rules he insisted must be maintained. He was very concerned that his employees were wholesome and be family-oriented role models. If any alcoholic beverage was found in an office, even a can of beer, that employee would be immediately fired. Walt wasn't too happy when the Swedish Representative, Gunnar Mansson, was declared "The most eligible bachelor in Sweden." Walt preferred his employees happily married and clean-shaven.

I was told a story about Walt giving a prince a tour of the Studio. He was introducing the animators and describing the process involved with creating animation cels. Special paints had to be used and were kept in refrigerators. Walt opened a refrigerator (as the animators are attempting to use sign language to say, "No, not that one"), only to show the prince the pile of sandwiches the employees had brought for lunch. One of the few times they witnessed Walt blushing.

People often ask me about Walt Disney and the stories they'd heard about how he ran the company. I was only seven years old when Walt died. I do know that as a child of a Disney executive I was treated with respect. That Walt truly loved children and felt their opinions were very important to the success of his company. From what I remember Father saying, the company felt like family. I only heard Father object twice to Studio policy. The first was Father's desire to grow a beard. As a compromise Father was allowed to grow a beard every presidential election year. The second incident was when Father named a cow "Lolita" in a comic book story. A character of that name in the Nabokov book did not convey Disney values. The name for the cow was vetoed.

My brother John had the opportunity to live by Walt's rules one summer when he worked at Disneyland. John's job was sales representative on Main Street in the Emporium. Disneyland employees had to follow very strict standards: No facial hair, no hair below the collar, and only appear during work hours in clean, Disney-issued, uniforms. John would drive to work, parking in the employees' lot. From there a guard would clock him in. He'd be handed a uniform to change into and proceed by underground tunnels in golf carts to his job location. If he needed a bathroom break or lunch he'd return to the tunnels where there were employee cafeterias. They were never to be seen in Disneyland Park itself eating or wandering away from their station in uniform. The tunnels or extra parking lots were called "backstage." This made the whole experience of attending Disneyland similar to attending a theatrical experience. The visitors were the audience and the workers were the actors who'd disappeared backstage after their shift. John was given a certain number of passes that he could use to enter the park as a visitor. Also "backstage" were the warehouses that held the extra merchandise for the stores, groceries for the food courts and supplies visitors did not need to see. It was all part of creating the "Happiest Place on Earth."

§

Chapter 11

Fields and Frogs

I have very little positive to say about my middle school. We'd moved from Burbank and my core friends to a new school where I knew no one. I wore thick glasses and my hair tightly tied back in a ponytail making my ears stick out. Boys on the bus would tease me mercilessly and poke me with straight pins. There were no brothers at my school that year to protect me or be a companion at lunch.

We moved to Thousand Oaks from Burbank because the smog in the Los Angeles area had become unbearable. Thousand Oaks had lovely fields and trails next to our new house which I enjoyed exploring. The schools and community were very conservative. I tried to fit in by playing sports. I played on the school soccer team, baseball team, basketball team and girl's tennis team. But my intelligence worked against me. Middle school boys didn't like smart girls. There were times my algebra teacher would have to leave the class and would assign me to teach. She said I knew the material as well as she did. This did not sit well with my peers. I ended up Valedictorian. This required giving a speech I wrote myself in front of all the school at graduation. This was not a privilege.

Mother did understand my dislike of middle school, and allowed me to stay home one day a week to be creative. I could read a book or learn a new recipe such as roast beef and Yorkshire pudding. I appreciated this opportunity to use the creative side of my personality and it helped balance the social mess that school was for me. I spent a good many days sewing my own clothes. I liked long cotton patchwork skirts. I'd wear these with a leotard or bathing suit so I was always prepared to jump in a swimming pool. I spent a few months making a custom quilt with each of the twelve squares representing things important to me. One square was friends' signatures, another a favorite poem, a frog, theatrical faces, etc. I'd embroider or appliqué each of the designs and then patchworked the whole quilt together. I entered it in the Ventura County Fair and was pleased when it won a blue ribbon.

Our house in Thousand Oaks was part of a model homes development. All the houses had the same floor plan with slightly different options on the flooring, look of the entrance, and location. The house Mother and Father chose was at the end of a cul-de-sac. We had open fields and ragged cliffs as our backyard. There were a few sets left over from movies such as *The Hanging Tree* that had been filmed here. We'd watch these frontier town fronts blow down in the Santa Ana winds that breezed in yearly. In the middle of these wheat and wildflower fields was a creek. Upon its banks I'd search for tiny tree frogs while trying to avoid the gopher snakes that also liked the frogs. After a good downpour my brothers and I would go in search of "the deepest mud." This wasn't just puddle splashing but looking for deep sticky mud holes. We found some that were waist deep. We would emerge looking like Creatures from the Black Lagoon. We washed ourselves off in the rain-swelled creek. It was then we thought, *fast moving water, I wonder if our rafts would clear the sharp rocks?* Only way to find out was to get the rafts. It was a thrilling ride. Before we knew it we had descended towards a large cement pipe that quickly went underground. This made for a tricky dismount. Fortunately, we all navigated out of the creek with skill and finesse. We decided not to tell Mother about creek surfing.

There was one hike from our house that dropped into a valley with cliffs on both sides. As I headed down this narrow dirt trail I saw in front of me a family of skunks. The mother was in front with five little ones following her. All with their tails held high in the air. It definitely looked straight out of a comic book but I took my time and waited patiently while this tribe found their way to the valley floor and a warm abode off the dirt trail.

We had two Siamese cats, Bonnie and Clyde. Bonnie was sweet and spent many hours on my lap. Clyde was a hunter—which included attacking me. There was a point when we'd have to neuter him or give him to someone to breed. We placed an ad in the paper and a couple wanted him. We drove miles and miles to drop him off at his new home. It was three weeks later that I heard scratching on the sliding glass door. It was Clyde. He'd found his way home over fields and through canyons. He was full of burrs and hungry. We now had to keep him and I had to accept the baby squirrels left on the doorstep as his way of saying "thank you."

We were all fairly good tennis players but not exceptional. Mother signed us up for a number of tournaments in the Santa Barbara area, two hours north of Thousand Oaks. If we won, we were to stay at a motel and eat at a restaurant. If we lost, we'd stay at a campground with a fire pit and eat hotdogs for dinner. The campground was on the beach in a town called Carpinteria. I wasn't very competitive in this setting and lost my matches in the first round. One brother wished he was better player; when he lost a match, he had a tendency to throw his racket. Mother did not tolerate this behavior. If he did it during the match she'd pull him from the tournament. We never did stay in a motel, but the beach was exquisite. We'd take our rafts out into the ocean waves. One year I swear there was a jellyfish convention right there at that beach. I was on my raft riding a wave in and travelling over at least twenty jellyfish. I had been stung by a jellyfish and it hurt. They say putting wet sand on it helps. It doesn't. Asking the cute lifeguard for medicine does.

If I wanted to be included in my brothers' activities I had to be ready to go at a moment's notice. They didn't allow time for combing hair, putting on make-up, or getting a sweater. "You can tie your shoes in the car." This is probably what led me to always having a packed backpack by the door ready to go.

As teenagers we had two favorite nighttime activities. The first was to organize a baseball game. There were fields that had lights that could be turned on by putting quarters into slots. It was a wonderful way to spend a warm summer night. A less respectable activity called tee-peeing was our other choice. Ten rolls of toilet paper was the cost and we were very successful at it. The challenge was to "decorate" a friend's house very late at night and be quiet enough not to wake anyone up—no giggling. If anyone heard any scurrying in the house instructions were to run to the car parked a few blocks away. Eventually, the victim would figure out who the perpetrators were and our house would be hit next.

That summer I went to a fine arts summer camp called Isomata. There I could sign up for art classes or theatre classes. I choose theatre. I somehow kept thinking I could work on the costumes or lights but, no, this was an acting class. For the final production we made our own costumes by tie-dyeing t-shirts orange and wearing them with jeans. The theatre script, *The New Chautauqua,* was composed of fairy tale vignettes. My monologue was about being a frog and ascending to the lap of a princess (the lap of a princess being the highest place any prince would ever want to ascend). The last day at camp parents arrived to pick up their kids and see the performance. I was nervous about this all week. It was only the smell of the tall pines that calmed me. My performance went well but it also confirmed my stage fright.

Living in Southern California we were never far from an earthquake fault line. It was early morning in Thousand Oaks when the bed started shaking back and forth. I thought this was great, just like an amusement ride.

Mother quickly poked her head in and demanded, "Get out of bed, away from that plate-glass window and stand under this door frame until I tell you to run out of the house."

Geez. I was having fun. This was called the 1971 San Fernando earthquake with a 6.6 magnitude. The only damage in our house was the art collection now hung a little tilted to the left providing us with a new skewed vision of the world.

For Christmas Grandmother Eleanor bought us a hang glider. This gave Mother the unique opportunity to tell four teenagers to "go jump off a cliff." On the little hill beside our house I did attempt to run and fly but I wasn't keen on attempting to glide off a high cliff. Having these rock cliffs almost in our backyard made Mother think if we wouldn't jump off then maybe we would fall off one and she signed us up for a rock-climbing course. Rock climbing when hiking or getting to the next cove at the beach is one thing. This was the other. The day came when we were "ready" to belay down the forty-foot cliff. I really wasn't enthusiastic about taking my life into my own hands. My brother Jim was the one working the safety rope from the top of the cliff. I was just supposed to nonchalantly lean over the cliff's side and walk my way down horizontally. Right. Let's throw out all that sense of balance we learned as a toddler to walk with gravity at our feet. I leaned back and took a few steps down the cliff before my foot slipped and I was at the mercy of my brother. Would he be paying attention and actually tighten the rope and save me from this death fall? I will admit I panicked dangling there in mid-air. I made it to solid ground and vowed I was never going to do that again, but I was grateful that Jim did his job very well.

We all had our nature creatures that we'd bring into the house. I liked to collect the little green tree frogs and had an aquarium full of them. My brothers caught a gopher snake. They had a cage for it as well but it demanded live food. They'd take *me* to the pet store to choose the mouse for the snake.

"No," I would tell them.

Then they'd say, "We'll choose this one."

"No, not that one. Look at its cute ears and sweet brown eyes. Choose another."

At this point I'd have to close my eyes and keep them closed until after we gotten home and the snake was fed. Mother also encouraged the wild to come inside. She fed the wild mice that lived in the pantry. I wondered, why couldn't these mice be caught and fed to the snake? We also attempted to catch blue belly and alligator lizards. This required making a noose out of a long strand of rye grass. We searched the rocks for a critter to capture without it losing its tail. We often caught them, but the alligator lizards bit. I preferred the blue bellies.

I had a best friend named Janice. She had a horse named Star. She would occasionally make the long ride from her house to the open fields next to mine. Together we went up into the cliffs. I didn't hike up there by myself. I was afraid of rattlesnakes, but we'd be high up on a horse. What we hadn't realized was the field terrain soon turned to desert plants and the worst were the jumping cacti. It is a clever design. This cactus has little fist-size balls piled one on top of another that easily leapt from their base to attach to any moving object. This included horses. When we got back, poor Star's legs were covered with this evil cacti. We couldn't just pull them off because they'd then embed themselves in our hands. It took a long time, carefully with leather gloves and tweezers, to remove all those spines.

Thousand Oaks was a five-hour drive from the Mexican border. We took a family trip that direction. We were most interested in purchasing an item not sold in the United States—firecrackers. Crossing into Mexico was hard for me. The hills of Tijuana were covered with cardboard houses where families lived in poverty. I wondered what happened when it rained. A little beyond Tijuana was Rosarito Beach, a sleepy town with a lovely Spanish-style hotel and great food. In the hotel lobby I'd sort through the muslin dresses embroidered with bright orange, green and red flowers often buying one. My brothers would search out the shop that sold bottle rockets, M80s and firecrackers.

Crossing back into the States the border patrol would ask if we had any pirotenicos and we'd innocently said, "No." *What are pirotenicos?*

Once home we'd wait for an occasion to light the bottle rockets or M80s. One night we set off quite a few bottle rockets when there came a knock on our door. Mother answered. A police officer asked if her teenagers had anything to do with the fireworks he'd been seeing.

"No, officer, not my children. They are good kids." Yeah, Mom.

It was spring in Thousand Oaks and the wild flowers were plentiful. I was on the bus coming home when I looked up the hill to where our house stood and thought I saw Father's Triumph smash into the cement barrier down the slope on the side of the house. When I arrived home, I saw it was smashed into the wall. How? Why? Walking in the door I saw my brother Jim with a towel over his head. Hum. Looks like Jim might have been involved, although he was acting in the play *You're a Good Man, Charlie Brown* as Charlie Brown. Maybe he was just rehearsing. Upon asking him it became obvious that he was not in a good mood. Mother wasn't home. I would have to wait to hear the story. Later when Mother got home, Jim was ready to explain the accident. He had the car out to wash and wax in preparation to take Lucy from the play to the senior prom. His foot slipped off the brake onto the clutch and the next thing he knew the car had slid over the embankment into the restraining wall. Jim didn't go to the prom. It took a mechanic six months to find all the replacement parts for the Triumph. "Poor old Charlie Brown."

I do have to confess there was one occasion when we might have crossed to the dark side. There was much talk amongst teenagers about this plant called marijuana. We decided to ask Mother how she felt about it.

Mom said, "I can't say yes or no until I've tried it."

One brother was able to obtain some seeds. These we planted, watered and watched grow into a bushy plant. While this was happening Mother put our house up for sale.

We asked Mom, "What to do with the plant?"

Mom said, "Put it in the bathtub, pull the shower curtain and if anyone asks call it a zinnia."

A new variety of zinnias were born that day.

When the weather was nice, Mother would pronounce, "Don't waste a beautiful day like this at school: Go to the beach."

Not wanting to be rebellious teenagers we did as we were told. It was a 45-minute drive to Zuma Beach and that was where we headed. Songs on the radio such as "Summer Breeze" by Seals and Croft, "Let's Go Surfing Now" by the Beach Boys and "Kodachrome" by Paul Simon reinforced this good decision. Some days we could even convince Janice's parents to let her come too. We'd bodysurf, picnic, hike, and lie in the sun.

Mother wrote an absence note for me the next day that read, "Please excuse, Cathy was kidnapped by pirates."

The school office responded, "Not excused."

I asked the attendance secretary to call Mother; she would verify it was an excused absence. The secretary refused and I had to live with an unexcused absence on my school record. This school had no sense of humor. I was not pleased. I was a straight "A" student not used to being penalized for something I was told to do. Mother and I started looking into alternative high schools.

I got contact lenses for my sixteenth birthday. A week later my brothers and I skipped school and drove to Oxnard beach. We'd rented a beach house there one summer and loved the sand dunes. I decided it would be too risky to wear my new contacts into the ocean. I proceeded to take a mirror out of my purse, set it on my towel, and began taking the first lens out. What I didn't know about contact lenses yet was how light and airborne they were. As I blinked it out of my eye it soared into the sand. I asked my brothers to please go buy me a flour sifter so I could look for the lost lens. They did. I sifted sand for many hours until the light left us. It was to no avail and a lesson was learned. I didn't get in trouble. Mother had other things on her mind.

§

Chapter 12

The Unexpected Foe

It was shortly after my glory days of elementary school that the silent Foe revealed himself. He was subtle. Fooled the doctors. Fooled us all. Started with a little thing. When I was eleven, Father said his rib hurt.

I said, "Mine hurts, too."

Two weeks later, two of his ribs had been removed. Mine were just ticklish and still are. Father's doctors' said, "The tumors was benign. Nothing to worry about."

After his operation I went to St. Joseph's Hospital to see him. In the corridor was Roy Disney, Senior, Walt's brother and partner at the studio.

Roy gave me a big hug and said, "I'm so sorry about your Father's tumor. I hope he recovers quickly."

I thought how kind and generous this person was to stoop down and acknowledge the emotions of a child.

Father was forty years old when the tumors in his ribs appeared. The Foe got trickier a year later. He hid the tumor deep in Father's hip. Tougher for the doctors to find and remove. The surgeon took out the tumor and part of Dad's hip. The hip was rebuilt with bones from his legs. This tumor was also declared benign. I hadn't been told about Father's first tumor in his abdomen when he was thirty. Why were his tumors reoccurring?

He tried to carry on. He'd go back to work at the Studio on crutches. An outing to Santa Anita Race Track had Mother holding her breath when the long-shot horse Dad had bet on began pulling up from behind.

Dad started jumping up and down shouting, "Go, go, go."

Not remembering his hip had just been replaced with two little leg bones.

It was after this surgery the doctors gave Father a new diagnosis of chemodectoma (now called paraganglioma), a very rare malignant cancer. There were only ten cases of this cancer on record—benign tumors returning. We were entering a dark tunnel with no light at the end. The cancer was attacking my father, my hero, my mentor, piece by piece. One wave of a wand and "Poof" my fantasy childhood was dissolving. Where were Super Goof, Professor Wonderful, or Mad Madame Mim? Couldn't they help?

Liver appeared on the dinner table constantly. The doctors ordered it to help Father regain his health. I hated liver. Ours was a household where you ate what was on your plate or you didn't eat. I didn't eat.

Living with a father with cancer caused a roller coaster of moods and emotions throughout the household. For five years we were on this ride. I don't like roller coasters in any form. They are shaky and unpredictable. They feel as if at any minute a wooden section will collapse, sending the cars plunging to certain death.

At first Father's tumors were fixable. Find one, surgically remove it, recover from surgery and life returned to normal. We always hoped after a surgery that this would be the last tumor. Father would go back to work. Then he started going to the Studio only three days a week and passing more of his workload onto his colleagues. Walking into our house after school I never knew what moods I would encounter. I walked on eggshells. I missed the middle school bus one day. My menstrual period had started and I wasn't prepared. I went home to change my clothes.

Mother exploded, "How could you miss the bus?"

I became very quiet, a dutiful daughter. God forbid I have any problems of my own. My escape was long walks in the fields surrounding our house. Here I could lie in a bed of flowers, look up at the sky, curse a god for the tumors, and eventually find myself breathing calmly again.

When I was fifteen, there was a day shortly after Christmas, the Christmas tree was still in the living room, when Dad woke up unable to move his legs. The nurse that helped out was called and it was determined Dad was paralyzed from the waist down. An ambulance took him to the hospital. He never came home. A tumor had grown in his spine and couldn't be removed. He was taken to the Motion Picture Hospital on Mulholland Drive in Woodland Hills where people in the entertainment industry went to retire with assisted-living privileges or in Dad's case to live out the next nine months of his life. Father never lost his humor or his hope.

Hospital policy said no children under sixteen years old were allowed. I was fifteen and Jeff was fourteen. The nurses had to sneak us in to see Father. I'd bring wildflowers I picked; orange poppies and purple lupine placed in coke cans for vases. I'd give them to Father and other patients on his floor. I talked to some fascinating patients. One woman claimed to be the first female reporter to have ever gone to Timbuktu.

She told me this story: "One morning we were woken very early and told to pack our things and leave. The natives were becoming restless and leery of the white man and I saw a few spears fly as we drove our jeeps out of town."

She gave me a grass necklace that she'd been given when there. The grass was woven into one-inch circles and these circles interlinked to form a long chain. I treasured it for years.

Even though Father was in the hospital, Disney was still sending him manuscripts to edit. Disney animators were working on the film *Robin Hood*. They gave Father a watercolor of *Robin Hood* characters catering to George in a hospital bed. The Studio was family. I have this painting in my living room today.

My teenage nickname was "Mad Converting Stomper." This was bestowed on me because of my tendency when angry to stomp up the stairs to my room and cry. I always hoped Mother would come in and ask what was wrong. She didn't. She was emotionally spent from her day at the hospital at Father's side. What happened to the "impossible"? I needed a fairy godmother that could do the impossible—make Father walk again. Also bring Mother home in good spirits and declare "Beach Weather." But the world wasn't a fairy tale. Cancer was cancer. A terrible villain the doctors didn't have the weapons to fight.

There is a day as children we discover Santa Claus is a myth not a real person. My brother told me when I was six. I wish he hadn't. We weren't told Father was dying. We could see it, the handsome witty man growing thinner and paler by the day. We could only do our best to be good children. Take responsibility for our needs. Hope Dad wasn't in pain. I wished for my mother back. She never really did return. I had only my own inner strength to call on. I hoped it was enough.

Visiting Father was hard. He was mentally alert, but his body was fading fast. The days of hope for a cure were long past. It is exhausting watching someone die. Being the only girl in the house I became responsible for cooking dinner for my brothers, washing up afterwards, and keeping the house neat and tidy. I had some favorite teachers at school, but they couldn't take away the fact that Father was dying or help me put dinner on the table.

§

Chapter 13

Holding Hands at Midnight

The summer I was sixteen Jeff, John and I were sent to Lewis and Clark College in Portland, Oregon, to take summer courses. Jim stayed home to help Mother and later celebrated his eighteenth birthday in Hawaii. I was angry at Mother for years thinking she just "didn't want to deal with the children" and Father at the same time. I later learned it was Father's request. He didn't want us to see him dying.

Jeff and I took art classes, while John, who was attending the college full time, took his chemistry requirements.

Wearing contact lenses instead of glasses showed off my high cheekbones. Guys were suddenly looking at me in a way I'd never experienced before.

Walking down the street young men would literally stop their cars and ask, "Where did you get that tan?"

On campus, students would turn their heads when I walked into a room. I was a California beach girl: Pretty, blonde, slim with a great tan.

I had my first boyfriend and first kiss. We'd spend summer nights holding hands and walking around this old estate transformed into a college campus. On really hot nights we would climb the chain-link fence surrounding the swimming pool and swim until the security guard showed up, unlocked the gate and escorted us out. There were other young men with whom I took walks and talked to late into the night. Finally, I was discovering what girls in a normal family experience.

The college was built around a stone manor house that faced Mt. Hood. There were lawns, fountains, rose gardens, and more lawns that reached down to the Willamette River all with views of that majestic mountain. I organized Sunday baseball games on the lower lawn while on the upper lawn, next to the manor house, a full-size orchestra played. It was during one of these baseball games we got the call that Father had died. Mother said there would not be a funeral, or memorial, and we were to stay in Portland. Even though we were expecting the call it was still hard when it came. I spent that evening in my boyfriend's arms crying.

It wasn't until I ordered Father's death certificate when I was in my forties that I learned where his ashes had been spread. It was off the beach in Santa Monica, where we'd gone swimming on the days Mother had called "Beach Weather."

Fifteen years after Father's death, his only sister, Ann, died of the same rare cancer.

§

CHAPTER 14

Sunsets and Suntans

Jeff and I flew home at the end of the summer session. Mother had already packed the house into moving boxes. There were some flowers in vases that relatives had sent. I wondered where Father's large collection of instruments had gone. Had Mother simply given them away? Mother had told Father's friends and colleagues that we were moving and she wasn't leaving a forwarding address. Mother didn't say a word about Father's death. It felt like we'd entered the Forest of No Return.

I did need a better high school and Mother loved the beach so we interviewed high-school principals up and down the California coast looking for a school that was innovative, creative, and trusted their students. We found a new one being built in Del Mar, a little town north of San Diego. This is where we moved. I don't know where Mother's income for the next years came from, but that wasn't a question I was allowed to ask. I presume there was a life insurance policy as well as Social Security payments. There was also quite a bit of Disney stock. Instead of a yearly raise, the Disney Corporation would offer a stock option that Father always took advantage of. In later years all four of us children graduated college, paid for with Disney stock.

Walt had told his employees, "The pay isn't great, but the benefits are."

Disney had paid all of Father's medical expenses.

Our condo complex in Del Mar was nicknamed "The Beehive." The shake siding had weathered from the original light brown to paper wasp gray. The land across from our condo was an estuary. It was a designated natural habitat for ocean birds, fish, and vegetation. If the ocean tides didn't ebb and flow through it, I'm sure someone would have built houses there as well.

I liked my new high school. The dress was casual, the teachers excited, and the subjects interesting. Surfing was one of the P.E. classes. I quickly became friends with Lisa, another student who'd recently moved to Del Mar from Washington, D.C.

I was lucky that this year it was my turn to drive the TR3, Dad's little white sports car, to school. The rule of our household was that the child who had most recently turned sixteen was the owner of the TR3 until the next brother or sister turned sixteen. I had long blonde hair that the wind whipped around as I drove. The car did have one fault. Anyone could start it with a paper clip. There were many days after school when I'd go to where I had parked my car and it was missing. Fortunately, no one ever stole it; just one of my friends had borrowed it and returned it to a different parking spot.

Father had always wanted me to play on the boys' tennis team. When I started high school at Torrey Pines, I skipped trying out for the girls' team and went straight for the Varsity boys' tryouts. The coach had no problem with a girl being on the team and I made the cut. Why ride on a bus full of girls to matches when you can ride on a bus full of guys? There was a glitch. We lived near San Diego and there were a number of military schools in our conference. When I showed up to play, cadets from these schools vehemently refused to play "a girl." They did have to forfeit the match, and I won by default but that wasn't why I wanted to be on the team. I wanted to play tennis and win the match fair and square.

A few blocks from our condo was a street with older homes and a large community hall. This building was usually boarded and locked, but a few nights a month the doors would open and live music would filter into the salty sea air. Lisa and I decided to investigate. We dressed in dancing attire and bravely walked in. There was a large wood floor similar in design to a skating rink with curved walls. It was German Polka Night. The regulars were delighted to have two young women join in the dance, and dance we did. I think every older gentleman, there weren't any young ones, desired at least two dances. Around and around we went. They weren't stingy about sharing their beer and we had quite a night of it. Our night to be the center of attention—like being Cinderella.

We lived a short walk from Torrey Pines State Beach. This was a long stretch of beach that was sided by multi-colored sandstone cliffs. I inherited my mother's love of the sea and every evening I'd go to the beach, sit in the sand in a flowing caftan, and watch the sunset. It made the transition and loss of Father easier. Rarely was I left alone. Most nights some male would sit beside me and introduce himself. I found talking to a variety of people gave me a broader perspective about how others lived. One night a dark-skinned man with tangled black hair insisted on "reading my palm." He talked about Aquarius in the East and Taurus in the West, but I really wasn't listening, I knew my life journey wasn't one that could be predicted in my sixteen-year-old palm.

Another evening a photographer gave me his business card and asked if I'd come to his studio for a photo shoot. He said he was legitimate and I could bring my mother, brothers, whomever I wanted to feel safe. I thanked him for the compliment, but said I'd rather be known for my intelligence than my looks. What other girls might have given for that opportunity?

There were the other "come back to my place for drugs or alcohol." Those I quickly put off. The one party I did want to attend was the end-of-the-season lifeguard event. I'd eyed the cute lifeguards during the summer and on the evening of this celebration two lifeguards came up to me to ask if I'd like to join them.

I said, "We'll have to walk up the hill and ask Mother."

Mother replied, "No."

Darn. I felt if we put our lives in the hands of these rescuers during the day I could trust them at night. She felt otherwise.

I think the hardest part about this move to Del Mar was living with a secret. Dad died of cancer. Mother felt this wasn't a topic to be discussed. Just smile and say everything's fine. Pretend it didn't matter. Pretend the past never existed. *Hush hush don't tell. Secrets secrets hide them well.*

John Denver's record *Rhymes and Reasons* I could listen to all night. I'd heard him perform live many times and liked the simple, heartfelt lyrics. That year my brother Jim went off to Lewis and Clark College and said I could borrow his record player. I'd put the record on and set it to repeat as I fell asleep:

"So you speak to me of sadness
And the coming of the winter
Fear that is within you now
It seems to never end
And the dreams that have escaped you
And the hope that you've forgotten."

One night I awoke to the smell of smoke. I found the record player on fire and my John Denver record melting. I kept thinking how was I going to write that letter to my brother explaining how I set his record player on fire. Maybe I could wait until he came home for summer. Yeah. Now that was a good idea.

We had a golden retriever dog named Addie Prey who loved to swim in the ocean. The quickest way to the beach was through Torrey Pines State Park. During the summer tent camping was allowed in this parking lot. It had signs reading "No Dogs Allowed." Dogs were allowed on the beach if I took the long way around. This path went through a field by some sandstone cliffs where the "druggies" hung out. I didn't feel safe taking that route which made me resort to ignorance. I'd take Addie through the State Park and hope no park official would stop me. Sometimes it worked and Addie could swim.

There were other frustrating days when a person in uniform would say, "No dogs allowed."

"Sorry, sir, I'll take her home straight away." Maybe if I put a hat and cape on her she wouldn't be considered a dog but a comic book character, "Addie of the Golden Fleece."

Many times I was invited by friends to join them at the beach in the middle of the night to look for grunions. Grunions are fish that lay their eggs in the sand. I didn't really believe they existed. I figured the phrase "let's go watch for grunions" was really an excuse to go to the beach in the middle of the night. I'd never seen any. It is also said that there is a scout grunion that goes to shore first and if it doesn't return then this beach isn't safe. I thought that was a great explanation for "Why didn't we see any fish?" One night, much to my dismay, the grunion did appear. They swam as far up the beach as they could then flipped and flopped until a hole was dug in which to lay their eggs. What I hadn't expected as they flopped back to the sea were the serious grunion hunters who began picking them up by the dozens and putting them in buckets. They were going to eat them.

I shouted, "Leave them alone." My voice could not be heard over the sound of the waves. I felt I was witnessing the impending death of hundreds of magical fish.

Del Mar has a lovely racetrack that runs for six weeks in late summer. The track was one-half mile from the beach and enjoyed daily temperatures of eighty degrees. Perfect weather to sit and watch the horses. Mom would put together a "pool" of $200 that we could use to bet, but all winnings went back into the pot. Of course, we could use our own money as well. If the pot was over $200 at the end of a day we'd go out to dinner, if it wasn't we'd eat at home. Mom would have me place bets for our group. Sometimes this meant putting $4 on horse number one, $2 on number two, $8 on number three, $2 on number five and $2 on number eight. It was embarrassing placing bets on so many horses when there was only going to be one winner. I wasn't legally old enough to place bets, but the management only seemed to care if I was cashing winning tickets. I left that for Mother to do.

Sometimes Lisa and I walked from the beach to the track. We'd get in free if we went to only the last two races—the eighth and ninth. The eighth race was the most prestigious of the day. We could easily find a discarded racing forum on the ground. Many celebrities owned horses in Del Mar and could be seen in the owner's circle. We never won big but we never lost big either. If we had a winning ticket we needed to find a friend or adult willing to cash it for us. I enjoyed the attention I received by wearing a bikini top with my beach towel wrapped like a pareo and showing off my tan.

Bandanas were popular. I could make a halter top out of one or a bikini out of two. To make a halter-top only required two machine stitches, one at the top (folding down the tip of the triangle) and another stitch along the fold. I threaded a cord through the top and another cord though the bottom seam, then tied them around my neck and back and I was set to go. Of course, it was important to double knot the ties because the high-school boys would accidentally try to untie them.

A swirl skirt is cut on a bias so it swings out far, but is narrow at the waist. I sewed one with white broad cloth alternated with red broad cloth. I'd wear this with one of my blue bandana halters. Did this make me the all-American red, white, and blue girl? Probably not—my belly button showed. I also made jewelry from a leather cord or waxed hemp, tied macramé style, intertwined with puka and other seashells I'd found on the beach. I wore no make-up. I wanted to be able to go swimming and not worry about what I looked like when I got out. My long blonde hair took a bit to untangle, but that was a price I didn't mind paying.

Most of my high-school friends lived in the town of Rancho Santa Fe known for expensive houses on acres of land. I was treasurer of the school club called AFS, American Field Service, which sponsored foreign students to come to America to study for a year and allowed American students the opportunity to live and study in another country. Having had foreign representations flow through our house as a child I respected other cultures and wanted to hear the stories the foreign exchanges students had to tell. We held meetings at various club members' houses. One night I went to give my girlfriend Diane a ride to an AFS meeting. She lived in a large mansion in Rancho Santa Fe because her father had recently married a wealthy woman. This house was huge. It had tennis courts, a swimming pool, two gardeners, a cook, maids, and a governess. Her parents were rarely home.

When I knocked on her door, Diane called out to me, "I can't get out of the house."

"Why not?" I said.

"The alarm system is on and I don't know how to turn it off."

Locked inside her mansion, what an interesting dilemma.

"Do you want me to go without you?" I asked.

"No," she muttered, "I'll set off the alarm, call the police and hope it won't cost my parents too much for another false alarm."

After a different meeting I was giving Lisa a ride home. The roads in Rancho Santa Fe can get very foggy at night. So foggy you can't see the road in front of you. I was in the TR3 and driving five miles an hour. I was worried another car might come up from behind, fast, and crash into us. Eventually, Lisa got out and walked the white center line so I could follow her and stay on the road. I didn't want to end up in the irrigation ditches that lined the street.

My senior year I had a new boyfriend. For Winter Prom I sewed a dress out of red velvet and lace from a picture in a history book of Queen Elizabeth I. I made up the pattern as I sewed. I booked a reservation at a French restaurant a few blocks from our condo. My boyfriend ordered escargot as an appetizer. I did try one—just one. It tasted like garlic. I was glad it didn't taste like snail. I was impressed they had fried the parsley garnish. The meal was delicious. The French tend to like to prolong mealtime and we finished with only 45 minutes left of the dance. We arrived at our school and frankly the grandeur of the dinner and my dress didn't fit the bland gymnasium location. Bleachers and basketball hoops just didn't fit my image of a royal ballroom. I was glad dinner took so long.

Mother liked to send us on adventures for birthdays. She felt new experiences were more important than material things. For my seventeenth birthday she arranged a surprise trip that included my friend Lisa, my brothers Jim and Jeff, a family friend, Scott, and myself. She'd booked us a condo in a little ski town in Utah. It was April and the slopes were empty. The weather was warm and I could ski in a halter-top. My brothers were better skiers and went further up the hill to the advanced trails. Lisa was skiing on the beginning slopes. I was an advanced beginner. The ski patrol had nothing better to do than escort me up in the chairlift and give me private skiing lessons on the way down. Everything was going well until the actual day of my birthday. I looked over to where Lisa was skiing and saw the ski patrol loading her onto a stretcher and carrying her down the mountain. Lisa was in great pain and we had to find a hospital. Lisa came out an hour later on crutches. No broken bones, only a dislocated knee. For the rest of the week it was the ski patrol and I on the advanced beginner slopes. I left Lisa in the condo with Scott who happened to be in a foot cast. He had broken his foot while escorting me to a barn dance a few weeks earlier. It appeared Sherman adventures were taking a bit of a toll on my friends.

Mother and I signed up for a class at the University of California, San Diego. It was a jewelry-making class. We were going to learn the fine art of cloisonné. It is a complicated art form. It involves shaping 1/16-inch thick silver strands into a design then adhering this to a silver backing. A thin paintbrush is dipped into the sand-like colored enamel and dropped into the cervices of the silver design. The jewelry piece is heated and the enamel melts. This process is repeated again and again to build the enamel up in layers until it crests the top of the silver strand. The piece is now lightly sanded with rough, wet sandpaper. Then with finer and finer sandpapers until the enamel itself is smooth and shiny. I loved my finished piece. It had a cobalt background, four petals of red with a yellow circle in the center—a fleur-de-lis. When I left for college a few years later, I took my pendant with me. I stupidly left it in the dorm-provided bathroom cubby. It was stolen. Even with lost posters plastered all over the campus I never saw it again.

§

Mother's way of saving time and water
with four children.

I loved my Pixie haircut.

Disney representatives would gather in our backyard. The children were always invited to join the conversation. Left to right: John; Wendall Mohler; Mother; Kai Pederson, Denmark; me; Mary Carey, Disney writer; Joy Granger whose husband was the Australian representative; and Peter Woods, London.

Everyone had to pitch in with chores. John and Jim were the chief bottle washers.

I was chief wine tester (or not, from the look in Mother's eyes).

John was the only one tall enough to possibly drive Dad's 1955 MG Roadster. Jim's on the left. I'm in the middle.

Off on a family excursion with matching outfits
that Mother had sewed.

A family outing to Uncle Jamie's
Beverly Hills swimming pool.

How did Mom keep her hair looking so
well groomed? I always came out of a
pool looking like a drowned rat.

Cathy in the Kimono
a Japanese representative
brought her.

Father at work in his office
at Disney Studios.

When visiting the Japanese representative Matsuo Yokoyama,
Father was invited to learn a dance from the Geisha girls.

We were heading off to Europe for the six-week tour promoting *The Jungle Book*.
John, Jeff, Jim, Cathy, Nancy and George Sherman, May 1967.

Cathy, Jeff, John and Jim outside The Rubens Hotel in London
with our friend the doorman.

Cathy feeding the pigeons on Trifalgar Square.

Father had to attend "formal" Disney representative meetings. This one took place
at "Le Mouton of Panurge" in Paris whose walls are decorated by Albert Dubout.
The representatives starting with the one with a "potty" on his head is Tony Bertini, Italy; on
his left two up is Horst Koblischek, Germany; two to the right is Andre Vanneste, Belgium;
the one with his arms around two beautiful women is Peter Woods, London, woman on his
left is his wife Barbara; my father, George Sherman, is standing saluting Barbara; and at
the head of the table half face is B. Van de Velde, Amsterdam. The rest are other representatives from publishing houses.

Dinner at our house in Burbank with the Italian Mondadori's children and our babysitters Gary and Sue Robson.

Jeff, Jim, John, Cathy, four mostly well-behaved children.

Young George pictured with his father Ransom Sherman, who was a popular radio and television personality.

Ransom's job in radio inspired Father to create his own sound effects studio. His sister Ann is peeking in on the show.

Grandfather Ransom was a radio personality. This photo of Mel Blanc, Dorothy Lamour, Ransom, and Bob Hope was taken before the taping of the radio program *G.I. Journal* episode #49, June 1944. *G.I Journal* was a weekly show recorded by the AFRS network for the American soldiers fighting overseas in World War II.

Father at the Studio with Dorothy Strebe, a newspaper comic strip illustrator and his writing partner Mary Carey.

Father shortly after his surgery removing a tumor from his hip. He returned to work using crutches to get around.

Left to right top row: Nancy, O.B. Johnston, George, an Irish lass that O.B. was sponsoring so she could gain citizenship, Jeff, Cathy, Jim, and John. Father is keeping his eye out for the representative we were meeting.

Atorrante and crew; Nancy, Jim, Jeff, Ron Powell, Lee and Rudy, heading from San Diego to Honolulu, July 2, 1975.

Cathy below decks during a race waiting for a spinnaker to fall through the forward hatch in need of packing.

Swiftsure to the rescue, "Send up a flare and we'll be there." On board is the crew of *Atorrante* and the crew of *Swiftsure* as they are approaching the finish line of the TransPac Race 1975. *Swiftsure's* crew; Nick Frazee - owner and captain, Blair Francis, Bob Haines, Ron Simpson, Jerry La Dow, Chuck Hope, Gary Gould, Scott MacLaggan and Fred Kirschner.

Mother's new boat, *Bohemia*, out in front rounding the buoy on the San Francisco Bay.

I was fishing with a drop line for dinner off the side of the boat.
I could catch the fish but I couldn't stand the thought of killing it.

Watching the Sunset every night on Torrey Pines Beach—how I kept my sanity.

My high-school senior portrait wearing the cloisonne necklace I had made.

Working on my tan in Del Mar.

May 1, 1982 marrying Brian at Mother's house in Boulder City, Nevada.
Lisa Welsh is my Maid of Honor. David Hogan is the Best Man.

Our honeymoon was driving the TR3 from San Diego to
Ashland and, as oft times before, there were a few
problems with the engine.

Chapter 15

Christmas Sailing

Mother bought a sailboat shortly after Father's death. She decided to take this opportunity when she had no responsibilities to sail somewhere in the world. The boat she bought was a 46-foot Cal32 designed by Nicholas Potter. It was slender in design, a racing boat with a wooden hull and teakwood decks. Its name was *Atorrante*. Jim, Jeff and Mother signed up for sailing lessons.

For the next few Christmases the family would sail to Avalon Bay, Catalina Island. We would find a Christmas tree, not too big, that we could tie with a rope to the stern of the boat. We made ornaments for the tree that might survive the ocean elements. After the first year of soggy paper stars and broken glass balls, we came upon the perfect dough ornament recipe. These we'd design, cook, paint and apply several layers of acrylic sealant. We now had a properly dressed Christmas tree.

It was basically an overnight cruise from our boat's slip to an anchor at Avalon, Catalina. We'd moor in the bay and stay four days including Christmas. We had a rubber raft that we used to get to shore. I'd explore the trails into the rugged mountains nearby. Once I hiked up a hill on the lush side in my flip-flops only to get to the top and find the other side of the mountain was a totally different terrain. It was cacti, thistles, and other plants with thorns. My feet were scratched and cut by the time I returned to the dock and could soak them in the ocean.

We would paddle our raft to a cove full of seals. The seals would surround the black raft out of curiosity. I worried one would flip the dingy over just for fun. I was afraid to swim in the ocean around Catalina. We'd been told countless stories, by those who like to frighten young children, that moray eels lurk in every rock crevice and we were sure to be bitten if we went swimming. Swimming really meant a quick dive off the boat and immediate return to it.

A sport we did partake in, called spinnaker sailing, required jumping into the ocean. The spinnaker is the colorful sail that bellows out in front of sailboats when sailing downwind. We set up our spinnaker with the boat anchored. We attached a rope seat to a line that went between the bottom two triangles of the sail. The top of the spinnaker was hoisted to the top of the mast. One corner end of the lower sail was on a lead rope in a "responsible" brother's hand. The challenge was to sit on the rope stretched between the two lower ends of the sail. The only way to accomplish this was to jump in the water, find the rope, sit on it, and hold on tight because once the wind came up you were at the mercy of the sail. There was some control with the lead rope in one brother's hand when pulled taut it would take the wind out of the sail. When the sail filled with air, you floated out of the water, similar to taking off in a hot air balloon. The only way to get off the rope seat was to jump down into the ocean. This can look very inviting and exciting when the winds are at peace with the world. When it was my turn, two things happened. I weighed less than my brothers and the wind picked up. I suddenly found myself 20 feet in the air, screaming at the top of my lungs, and there was nothing I could do but hold on. My brothers could have pulled the lead rope taut, but they were too busy laughing. The moment the wind died just a little, I jumped. I now knew when not to trust my brothers.

I was fishing off the side of the boat, one evening right before dinner, when much to my surprise I caught a decent size fish. I liked to fish for the dramatics of it. I looked cool in my straw hat and little drop fishing line hooked with cheese.

Mother said, "Great, your dinner. I have the barbecue all ready to go with hamburgers."

I was a vegetarian who would eat fish, but I couldn't bear to kill the poor thing. I felt sorry enough it had a hook in its mouth. I think growing up in a comic book world made me feel all living things can potentially talk and I wasn't about to deal with the wrath of this ocean fish. I set it free. I told Mother I was much more in the mood for an omelet.

The boat had a gimbaled stove. This was important for when the boat was sailing on a reach or into the wind because it would heel from left to right. The gimbals on the stove kept it level no matter how the rest of the boat was tilted. No one wants a pot of boiling spaghetti noodles spilling onto the cook. The dining table also was gimbaled allowing a crew to eat without plates sliding into their laps. At night the table would fold down and locked into place allowing the previous seats to become two more sleeping berths.

Mother liked to cook calamari. She'd buy a big frozen box of it and put it in the boat's icebox. I always hoped she'd forget and we'd have to throw it overboard to feed the creatures of the ocean who greatly appreciated squid. At the same time Mother was very good at keeping fruits and vegetables fresh. She'd wrap an almost ripe fruit in tin foil. This kept them from ripening further. She always had a stash of avocadoes that I considered life's ambrosia.

The second Christmas we did our usual preparations, and Mother asked my brothers at least three times if had they filled the propane tanks which fueled our stove while sailing.

"Yes, Mom, of course," said the teenage boys.

It is Christmas Day and Mother managed to fit a full-size turkey into the boat's little icebox. She basted, stuffed, added potatoes and put it in the oven to wait the five hours until dinner could be served. About an hour into the roasting she checked the turkey and noticed it was barely cooked. The oven had no heat. The boys had not filled the propane and there was not a propane outlet on Avalon.

Mother told me, "You and I are going to shore."

We paddled our way to the pier and surveyed what options were available. Since it was Christmas most of the town was closed. On a side street we found an old coffee shop that was open, serving Christmas dinners to the locals.

Mother walked up to the owner and asked, "Can you do us a very big favor? If we rowed our half-cooked turkey ashore, would you be kind enough to put it in your oven and finish cooking it for us?"

He was feeling the Christmas spirit and agreed.

Mom and I went back to the boat, grabbed the turkey and in the little rowboat took it to shore, up this hill and into the coffee shop. The owner placed the turkey in his oven and thankfully Mother didn't go over the line and ask if we could bake a pumpkin pie as well. Mom and I (I'm not sure why my brothers, who were to blame, got out of helping us solve this problem but they did) rowed back to shore four hours later to pick up a perfectly cooked turkey. Mother found a liquor store open and bought a bottle of their finest whiskey to give the restaurant owner in payment for his generosity. We are now walking down the streets of Avalon with cooked turkey aromas filling the air while passing more than a few rugged, homeless-looking people on the street. I would gladly have given the turkey to them, but Mother was determined to have a family Christmas dinner. Down the dock we trotted and into the rubber raft. Any of you who have stepped into a rubber raft will appreciate the complexity and agility that is required to do this with a whole, hot, cooked turkey in one's hands and not have the turkey nor oneself plop into the sea.

The rest of the evening went well and there were turkey sandwiches for the rest of our stay. Of course, a cup of hot coffee was hard to come by. Mother and I would trek back to the coffee shop for coffee and pie and continue our heartfelt thank yous.

§

CHAPTER 16

Ocean Obstacles

That was the Christmas before the really big adventure. I had arranged with my high school to take a semester off while getting credit by writing about my experiences as we sailed. This way I could graduate in June with my senior class. We were taking our boat, *Atorrante*, to Hawaii and then the South Seas. This was Mother's response to Walt's philosophy, "If you can dream it, you can do it." Mother and I spent every weekend gathering supplies. There were emergency kits to provision. We scoured Army surplus stores and bought canned water, and filled toothpaste-type containers with peanut butter. We made sure that the life rafts would inflate and the flares would fire. We even practiced shooting a few flares one night on the bay. There were tins of meat, foil-wrapped fruits, soup, crackers, and lots of medicinal gin and tonic. The crew consisted of my two brothers, Jim nineteen, Jeff fifteen, a college friend of Jim's Ron, two hired crew, Rudy and Lee, and one last slot to fill. Mother and I flipped a coin for who would crew the boat to Honolulu and who would fly over and meet the boat there. I lost the coin toss. Mother timed the boat crossing to be during the Transpac Race. The Transpac is a bi-annual race from Los Angeles to Honolulu. There are usually around sixty boats that enter the race. Racing that year was Roy Disney, Jr., on his boat *Shamrock*, who was the one who'd suggested to Mother to sail during the Transpac so if there were any problems there would be other boats in the area. On July 2, 1975, our boat set sail from the San Diego pier headed for Honolulu. I watched it sail out of sight and for some reason I cried. I don't usually get emotional, but I cried.

I had two weeks before flying to Hawaii to meet the boat. Lisa and I decided to visit college campuses up and down the California coast. We were two young females off on a road trip. We first visited UC Santa Barbara, where Lisa chose to go to college. We headed further north to UC Santa Cruz, a lovely wooded campus where we stayed the night in the dorms. It was the next day we heard this news bulletin: "A boat sailing to Hawaii has sunk." I wasn't worried, but Lisa said I should call the Coast Guard. I did. I asked the name of the boat and they told me it was the *El Capitan.*

I said, "Great," and hung up. "See, Lisa, nothing to worry about."

We toured Stanford, a school I was interested in. We were driving over the Bay Bridge to visit UC Berkeley when another newscast came on the radio. This time they said that a boat had sunk in the middle of the Pacific Ocean and its name was *Atorrante.* Wait. That was our boat. I panicked. Lisa pulled over and I called home where my oldest brother John was. He said the story was true. The reporters had just left, but that everyone had been rescued.

I wasn't one to sit still and told Lisa we needed to turn around immediately and head back to Del Mar. I wanted to know the whole story. John told me this: The boat was halfway to Hawaii. Jim and Ron were on deck. It was midnight and the ocean was perfectly calm. Then it hit. The bow of the boat rose in the air, and the hull was splintered.

Mother's journal had exact details: *"Jeff and I were on 2 a.m.-5 a.m. watch so were in bed early in the forward cabin. Ron and Jim were relieving Rudy and Lee at 11 p.m. but Rudy was still on deck with Jim and Ron when it struck—no one checked watches but it was about 11:25 p.m. They heard it hit, and it pushed the boat to starboard. They saw its large rounded smooth shiny shape surf alongside the cockpit port and heard its exhalation. Its strike into the hull and the immediate sound of rushing water awakened me in the forward port berth. I yelled at Jeff and in the 5-6 seconds it took to get my feet on the floor the bilge boards were floating and I was standing in a couple inches of water. Ron and Jim were below by then. We put Lee at the helm. Jim got on the radio. He raised the Coast Guard in San Francisco and Long Beach within 15 minutes who asked all sorts of irrelevant questions along with the vital ones. Roy E. Disney on* Shamrock *and Nick Frazee on* Swiftsure *both saw our flares. I launched them from the cockpit and although we had tested both guns and flares I had never used a flare gun and had a hellish time figuring out how to break it open for shell insertion. It also has quite a kick. Ron had immediately inverted the strobe waves on the life rings which* Swiftsure *also saw.* Swiftsure *was closest so told* Shamrock *they would come. Meanwhile Rudy and Ron inflated the rafts, brought out emergency duffels, water, etc. By now* Atorrante *was waist deep with water in the cabin. We loaded the life raft with the sextant, zenith, some of our wallets, checks, passports, blankets which was silly but did come in handy on* Swiftsure *and Ron's mandolin. Jeff, bless his heart, was still trying to save her. He had gotten the #1 genoa that was down on the foredeck and was trying to wrap it around the hull, but that gorgeous long keel made it impossible to touch the hull at the vital point. Jim and Jeff and I were last off. The boys refusing to leave until the guys from* Swiftsure *became so frightenly insistent. When we got in the life raft,* Swiftsure *was only about 50 feet off our port and* Atorrante *was showing about 2 inches of freeboard.*

I asked the captain, Nick, if I could stay on deck and watch. When there was less than 1 inch of freeboard and her decks were awash, I felt myself disintegrating and someone took me below. They handed out beer and dry clothes, smoothed out the sail bags in the forward cabin and let us cry it out. They all said later they doubted if any other boat in the race was as well equipped or prepared for an emergency at sea."

When Nick radioed Roy Disney, Jr., the next day to say the rescue went well and all were safely onboard before *Atorrante* sank, Roy, Jr., was shocked to hear it was our family and glad he'd advised Mother well on when to make the crossing.

The Coast Guard called Mother and asked only one question, "Did you hit the whale or did the whale hit you?"

Mother retorted, "I didn't stop and ask it."

The boat was not insured for the crossing, but was insured for the islands where most boats run into danger with coral reefs or sandbars. I again couldn't sit still and got on a plane to Hawaii. I'd never been afraid of flying, but this time I looked down at that vast amount of ocean and I cried. I cried out of pure fear. Not because of what happened but because of what could have happened. I was seventeen and again on my own. I checked into a hotel, but didn't sleep and didn't eat. I just sat on the dock for three days waiting for Mother and my brothers to appear. I did talk to the Harbor Master and on the third day he said to expect them tomorrow. They did appear, along with helicopters and media boats. I'd never been so relieved in my life.

Mother's journal: *"We came on deck just before the finish with a 1.5 oz rainbow spinnaker up. The time was 4:15 p.m. A beautiful evening and our first intimation of the 'press': Press boats, helicopters, escorts, two-pressmen were in the harbor plus Transpac officials. They sent a message I was to 'Report to the Coast Guard Promptly!'*

"We pulled into a slip where wives, girlfriends and Cathy (so good to see) were loaded with leis and t-shirts emblazoned with: "Swiftsure to the rescue: Just send a flare and we'll be there." There were also barrels of mai tais. I suddenly panicked. I asked if there was any 'Jack' left and Blair handed me a drink that must have been 6 oz. Jack Daniels and 2 oz. water. Transpac PR man Nick said 'no press' until Jim and I wanted—so behind the gate they waited. There was no way out. I let Jim do the talking and he was great. Roy Disney, Jr. came over and gave his condolences. We walked down to Hawkeye and commiserated with Burke former owner of Atorrante.

"Finally all of us a bit more than half 'sunk' gathered up our circumspect gentleman navigator who had gotten us to Hawaii and escorted him to his hotel room. A funnier sight I have rarely seen. We marched single file through the streets of Honolulu from the yacht harbor to the Halekulai in our Swiftsure *shirts, cast-off shorts, barefoot, and possessions in plastic bags. Jim trying vainly to keep order: 'All right, survivors, single file now, let's be dignified, keep it cool.'* Swiftsure's *navigator was staggering back occasionally to ask Jeff if he still had the rubber bands around his duffel. Cathy, every 20 feet or so, putting her finger to her lips and saying, 'Sssh,' which was immediately echoed by the rest. We are next sitting in a circle on the floor in the*

lobby of the Halekulai trying not to giggle. We then went to dinner on the terrace—all barefoot and shipwrecked."

I learned many lessons from this experience. First, newspapers, radios, and even the Coast Guard often have their facts wrong. Second, when all was said and done it didn't matter we'd lost a $100,000 boat and all the personal belongings it held—Mom, Jim and Jeff were safe. Third, as I sat on that Honolulu dock for three days not telling anyone who I was: the stories, gossip and out-and-out lies I heard were incredible. It made me never want to judge anyone until I'd heard all sides of the story. And the comic book world of the impossible, a whale sinking a boat, could actually happen—at least to my family. Fortunately, this adventure did have a Disney ending.

Mother was organizing a banquet for the crew that rescued her. The next morning we couldn't find Jim and Ron. We wrote a note and pinned it to a palm tree. In my world this was a "normal" procedure. They found the note. We went from jewelry store to jewelry store collecting twelve silver cups, each jewelry store only having two or three cups in stock. When we finally had bought twelve, we needed to find someone who was willing to engrave the cups with the crew members' names. A beautiful Chinese lady said she could do it immediately. There were still TV reporters all over the island we had to avoid. The banquet went well and *Swiftsure's* crewmen were genuinely impressed with their engraved cups.

A few weeks later, the Transpac Committee awarded Nick Frazee a special award: *"Of considerable interest to the Committee each year is the award of the Stephen Newmark Seamanship Trophy. This year,* Swiftsure *not only won the trophy for her achievement in the rescue of the yacht* Atorrante *(not an entry), but at the Trophy Dinner, won a standing ovation from all of the yachtsmen and crew. This was probably the greatest award any skipper could receive— a tribute from fellow yachtsmen for competent handling of a rescue operation. Thanks, Nick Frazee."* —Commodore Hays McLellan.

From Honolulu we went to the island of Kauai and spent three weeks in Hanalei Bay. Mother recuperated and I explored the beaches and Wainiha cliff trail that I found stunning. I hiked barefoot to the waterfall and swam in its pristine pool of water. I still hoped to one day make it to Tahiti.

For years there were times one of us would say, "Have you seen my blue sweater, favorite turtleneck, some book . . ." only to then remember, it was on the boat.

Mother came home and proceeded to buy a 48-foot aluminum-hulled boat named *Bohemia* that a whale could only dent not sink. We couldn't get insurance for it on the open ocean. *I wonder why?* We were allowed to sail it up and down the California coast. These restrictions kept Mother from attempting another crossing to the South Seas, but didn't hinder us from many more adventures.

§

CHAPTER 17

Bohemia Will Only Dent

Sails are similar to knitting needles. If you have fine thin yarn you need to knit with thinner needles. If the yarn is thick you use thicker knitting needles. The spinnaker on a boat comes in thin fabric for when the winds are slight and gauged up by .5 oz. increments. Thicker fabrics are used for stronger winds. The boat goes fastest on the lightest weight sail that can handle the wind. Thus, the more sails on board, the better chance to reach that optimum speed. Unfortunately, like the rest of us, sails grow old, develop stretch marks, sag where you don't want them to, and generally lose their strength. In sailing parlance, they get "blown out," meaning they have lost their shape of youth. An old sail has little resale value, but was quite dear initially. Not wanting to throw them away, but too old to use, they gather dust in some corner of the garage or, for very large boats, in sea containers. An old warhorse of a sailboat accumulates plenty of sails; *Bohemia* fit that bill, with thirty sails, some of very dubious quality.

The balloon-like, downwind sails, spinnakers, are fabricated from a light fabric, weighing just .5 oz/square yard used for the lightest of breezes, .75 oz medium wind, 1.5 oz heavy air, and 2.25 oz. If you have the 2.25 up, it's generally because something disastrous happened to the 1.5, it's still quite windy, and you have not yet come around to your senses that you would be better off with a jib rather than a spinnaker.

Bohemia's .5 oz spinnaker had a lot of miles, and the fabric was quite worn. We joked that it was probably a .25 oz, and let about as much wind through it as it stopped. In the cold dark of the early morning of an overnight race, the offshore breeze filled in quite suddenly. Just as quickly the poor sail blew out, shredding along many seams, leaving streamers fluttering in the darkness.

I wanted to use the fabric. I designed a quilt I would sew for Jeff. I went by North Sails, a custom sail shop, and asked for scraps of spinnaker cloth. They happily gave me a bag full. This allowed me more colors to design with. The quilt turned out soft and lovely. Unbeknownst to me, Jeff was secretly designing and sewing me a kite from the same ripped spinnaker cloth. We exchanged these gifts that Christmas.

One of my jobs when racing the boat was below decks. When the spinnaker is taken down, the sail is stuffed into the forward hatch, dumping it into the cabin. I had to untangle the sail and get it ready to be hoisted again when needed. One procedure for packing a spinnaker is to lay the sail out, top to bottom, gather the fabric together, and rubber band or tie with light yarn the cloth every few feet, creating something that looks like a long snake. In a perfect world, the sail is fully hoisted still banded making it a much easier job, the bands are then broken by pulling on the sail's corners, at which point the sail fills and the boat accelerates.

Packing the spinnaker isn't always fun. On wet, windy days, the sail is soaked, and those packing the sail get soaked as well. Usually after a spinnaker is dropped the boat switches to an upwind course, where the sails are pulled in tight and the boat pointed as close to the wind as possible while still maintaining speed. If it is at all windy, sailing upwind causes the boat to tip and heel over, while below-decks the spinnaker and I would go sliding towards the low side. Once I had settled back to the job at hand, "those in command" would decide to tack; the boat would turn with the sails filling on the new side, heeling the boat way over the other way, with the sail and me sliding across the cabin the other direction. This tacking back and forth had me below decks feeling like a ping-pong ball.

The lines that hoist the sails up the mast are "halyards," and for a racing boat there can be quite a collection; one for the mainsail, two jib halyards, plus two spinnaker halyards. Occasionally, the halyards get tangled. This necessitates someone going to the top of the mast and trying to straighten them out. A chair, called a boatswain's or bosun's chair, is attached to a halyard. The volunteer sits in the chair and is winched up the mast. There was a day at dock that Mother was giving everyone the opportunity to try out the boatswain's chair.

I was about halfway up the mast before saying, "That's enough, I'll come down now and how about that gin and tonic?"

A very popular Southern California sailboat race is from Newport to Ensenada, Mexico, which usually takes about a day. We gathered a crew together of family and friends and headed south. One thing about ocean racing in Southern California is the fact that there are times, particularly at night, when there is no wind. Seagulls and cormorants drifting on the surface would pass us. And since the rules allow no motoring, all we could do was calmly wait, tell a few jokes, make a small sacrifice to the wind gods with just a splash of Jack Daniels (we might need more later), and work on that inner patience. This being called "a race" allows for lots of patience practice and *I can't control this so let go of any vision of winning.*

We did eventually arrive in Ensenada. The streets were full of crews. You can identify each boat's crew by their matching polo shirts. Even I spent a few evenings embroidering

"Bohemia" on the backs of navy-blue polo shirts and the crews' names over the front pocket. Lisa was with me. She was still on crutches from her last Sherman adventure. As we were walking down this crowded street to the local watering hole, we saw my brother, Jim, walking ahead of us, suddenly get whisked away in a Mexican police car. Not what you'd want to call home and tell Mother. Lisa and I asked the first policeman we encountered where the police station was located. Fortunately, Lisa took Spanish in school and didn't learn her sense of directions from a cereal box like I had. We did have to hobble there slowly. When we reached the police station, Jim had already been released. Another crew member, Robbie, tan and blond, had walked in with a bottle of Jack Daniels under one arm and a bottle of tequila under the other and politely informed the police that Jim was not part of the other kids drinking on the streets, the reason the police pulled the group over. Lisa and I then had to ask directions to Hussongs, the bar in Ensenada where we assumed everyone would land sooner or later. When we arrived at Hussongs, there were policemen outside the door checking IDs. This was new. They'd never checked IDs before. Lisa and I were seventeen. The drinking age in Mexico is eighteen. But wait; there was Rudy who'd been filming the race from our boat for the late night news.

He winked, and asked the policemen, "Could you move over just a little where the light is better so I can film you for American TV?"

He hand signaled us to slip in. We did. It worked. Dos Equis beers were ordered and other crew members were already there, as well as many cute guys from the other boats. When we arrived home that night, by car, we watched the newsreel that Rudy put together "for American TV." We were glad to see the sequence of our entering Hussongs had been edited out.

Nick Frazee, the owner and captain of *Swiftsure*, the boat that rescued Mother and brothers when *Atorrante* sank, also was Commodore of the San Diego Yacht Club and offered to sponsor us to become members. We were accepted. As a seventeen-year-old this meant a male-dominated place to prance about, and I did. There were regular activities that added to my social calendar. One was the Wednesday Night Beer Can Races. This was an informal race beginning at 6 p.m., sailing to a buoy, rounding it and heading back to the yacht club. At first there was the added element of boats being equipped with water balloons and launchers to take an innocent shot at their otherwise serious competitors. This became outlawed when someone realized broken balloons weren't good for the ocean ecosystem. That only left cheating. There were a few ways to cheat. First was crossing the starting line before 6 p.m., next was turning before the buoy, and last was turning on the motor. After the races the clubhouse sponsored a barbecue dinner on the deck with liters of free wine.

There is something rather refreshing about being soaking wet. Yet there are times when this is more embarrassing than cleansing. Such was the case when we'd sailed the boat on the weekly beer can race and as I jumped off the boat with line in hand to secure the boat to the dock I found myself a foot short and in the bay. Right. I felt a little like Goofy. Wet and embarrassed with no change of clothes, I had to carry on projecting wet as just my style.

A few years later, when I was in college, there was one very cold evening and I was feeling homesick. Then I remembered, it was Wednesday, beer can races had gotten into my blood.

My brothers were allowed to take the boat out on their own as long as they had Mother's permission. It was Spring Break and we decided to visit the Todos Santos Island off the coast of Ensenada, Mexico. It is basically a rock island populated by seabirds. We anchored in the little cove. We hiked on the rugged rock island. Birds were swooping down at my head at every turn. I hadn't known how seabirds would attack humans to protect their ground nests. After our hike we were preparing dinner when it started to rain and the winds picked up. Strong winds. Winds that could send a boat crashing into the rocks. We knew we needed to head back to San Diego and Jeff began pulling on the anchor. It wouldn't budge. He felt the only way to get it up was to get in the rubber raft and go to shore where he could pull the anchor from another direction. I saw my brother in this raft with these heavy seas coming in thinking *why don't we cut the anchor rope and go*. Eventually, Jeff freed the anchor and was back on board, but the winds were pushing the boat towards the rocks. Please let the boat's motor start this time. The engine started and we made it back to San Diego. Since we'd been in Mexican waters we had to wait at the Coast Guard dock for inspection before going back to our berth at the yacht club. We arrived after hours and had to spend the night at the Coast Guard dock. Part of sailing was knowing when to pull anchor and head to a safe port.

Red Tide is a condition when the ocean has an outbreak of algae. Phytoplankton blooms cause the water to turn a red or brownish color. These blooms are also fluorescent. It isn't healthy to swim during a red tide, but on the boat the water in the head (toilet) is pumped in straight from the ocean. We'd spend an hour flushing the toilet and watching this drug-free psychedelic show. Isn't it interesting where you can find free entertainment?

When I turned thirteen, Father gave me a moonstone. It is a semi-precious stone that he'd "smuggled" into the country from India. I always like the image of a Disney executive with this stone in his sock going through airport customs. Mother took me to a jewelry designer to have it set in gold. I loved this necklace and wore it daily. After sailing one evening I felt for it and it was missing. I tried to stay calm while we did the after-sailing chores. We had to rinse off the sails and wash the salt water off the decks and hull. As I was turning off the fresh water spigot, I looked down and there was my moonstone. It was literally an inch from falling between the dock boards into the bay. I was so glad to retrieve it safely. I still treasure it today.

§

Chapter 18

Food Is My Enemy

My journey into anorexia began after two tragedies and a teenage power struggle with Mother. Father's death and the boat sinking affected my sense of safety. In my crumbling adolescence I decided food was the one thing I could control. I could fight hunger and not eat. Simple concept, easily executed and it worked. I could envision all food as my enemy. The three days on the dock in Honolulu proved I didn't get hungry. I could survive without eating. I proceeded down a lifetime path.

There was a day my senior year in high school when Mother gave me an ultimatum, "If you want to play on the boys' tennis team a second year, you have to eat breakfast."

I responded, "Fine, I won't try out for the team."

I gradually cut food groups out of my diet. The first to go was butter, cream, and fats. Next were carbohydrates. I lived mainly on fruits and vegetables. Don't all the health books say this is what we need more of? For energy I was addicted to diet soft drinks with caffeine. I could have easily been the poster girl for Diet Pepsi.

The only food issues I remember pre-high school were Mother's adventurous cooking and household rule that you couldn't be excused from the dinner table until you tried three bites of whatever she'd cooked. Have I mentioned I was stubborn? I'd often look at her home-cooked meal with the incredulous thought of *Did you really think I'd eat that*, the cottage cheese looking stuff in the lasagna, and liver. Why did a perfectly good salad need to be topped with anchovies? My preferred method of getting out of eating dinner was to fall asleep at the table. Eventually, she'd have to send me to bed. Other than that my childhood was filled with homemade popsicles, ice cream, and penny candy.

The experts say that the propensity to becoming anorexic is usually grounded in a personality type formed at birth. Besides the need to get straight "A's," I remember a few other obsessive qualities. I'd save my Halloween candy, for years. At first I only wanted to have more than my brothers, later because I was trying to set a record.

Mother told me, "You were the only child I ever knew who had to be first in line in kindergarten."

Frankly, I didn't remember that. I did remember knots in my stomach during the last period of the day in middle school and high school when I had to take the bus home. I did want to be first in line. I didn't want to get stuck in the back where I was mercilessly teased. In high school I wanted to save a seat for Janice. Those weren't the only firsts I had to be. I also had to be the best on every math test in elementary school—although my elementary report cards did have a few comments such as "respect for authority," satisfactory (not excellent), maybe because I knew a better answer than the teacher.

I began taking birth control pills when I was seventeen. It wasn't because I was sexually active; I'd hardly kissed a guy. It was because the anorexia had stopped my menstrual periods. The birth control helped regulate my hormone levels and brought back my periods, *like I really wanted them back?* My boyfriends would have loved to know I was on birth control, but I didn't tell them. I wasn't ready for sex.

I was obsessed with getting "A's" in school and desperately wanted to be high-school Valedictorian. I wasn't. My chemistry teacher gave me a "B+" in her class. It wasn't because of my test scores. It was because I walked around barefoot. She required shoes in her classroom. I'd have to hurry back to my locker, get my flip-flops, and return to class tardy. In retrospect, I can see how shoes should be required around chemicals and broken glass, but my feet had calluses from months of walking on hot sand. What are a few shards of glass to a teenager? She graded me down for being tardy. My good friend Diane's GPA earned her the honor of Valedictorian leaving me with 2nd place, Salutatorian. I felt I'd let myself down (just a little).

The Del Mar years were fraught with anguish. Mother had extreme moods and I never knew after school what state of mind she'd be in. She'd sometimes call from the yacht club telling me to have dinner cooked and on the table at 6 p.m. I figured if I was not eating then maybe it wouldn't be my responsibility to cook dinner, re-enforcing my anorexia.

The ultimate in my being an anorexic came one day while I was sunbathing on the beach.

This older man stopped by my towel and asked, "Can I take your picture?"

I answered, "For what purpose?"

"I teach anatomy at the university and I can see every bone in your body," he replied.

The anorexic in me took this as a compliment, not an insult. I let him take pictures.

§

Chapter 19

Sailing in San Francisco

My sixteen- and seventeen-year-old summers had been full of drama and loss. What in the world would the summer I turned eighteen bring? It started with sailing the new boat, *Bohemia,* to San Francisco. We stopped at many lovely ports on the way up the Californian Coast. Santa Barbara is always beautiful. Pismo Beach had a reputation for being uninspired, but I found it delightful. Their yacht club consisted of a picnic table and restrooms. There was a shop that sold hand-spun wool three blocks from the dock. I bought some yarn and taught myself to knit a watch cap. We traveled the next day past the old canneries of Monterey. Having read John Steinbeck's book *Cannery Row*, I found them eerie in their abandoned state on the edge of the sea. I imagined the generation of fishermen who made their living working these docks. They were now deserted buildings ready to topple into the unforgiving ocean.

We arrived at the San Francisco Yacht Club in Tiburon across the Bay from downtown San Francisco. What makes a good yacht club isn't what most people think. It is easy access to the bathrooms to brush ones' teeth first thing in the morning. It needs to be within walking distance of a laundromat and some sort of grocery store. Swimming pools, tennis courts, these don't matter, but having clean towels and socks do. The San Francisco Yacht Club was ideal. It didn't have a dress code. If I desired a sandwich from their dining facilities I could show up in boat attire: Cut-off shorts, a bikini top, and wind-blown hair. Belonging to the San Diego Yacht Club gave us reciprocal rights. We were allowed to dock at other yacht clubs for a nominal fee. We docked there for two months.

Tiburon was small and quaint with friendly people. I liked taking morning walks on narrow paths that wove through the hill neighborhood of Belvedere. Everyone I passed gave a cheerful hello. We spent our days exploring Angel Island, a little island in the middle of San Francisco Bay, where detainees were quarantined. The old buildings still existed and gave a stern picture of years gone by. A deer population had overrun the island and begged for snippets from our picnic.

At night we'd turn the radio to the show *Mystery Theatre*. We felt the dramatic lure that old-time radio shows had on the masses before television was invented. The soft rocking of the boat as I lay in a narrow berth and the sound of the halyards knocking against the mast lulled me to sleep.

We'd sail out to watch the sailboat races. There was one major race going on called the Big Boat Series. I'd fly the kite Jeffie made me off the stern of our boat—much to the dismay of the serious racing sailors. I had a boyfriend, Steven, who was crew on one of the boats racing. That boat was called *Whistle Wing V* owned by Hastings Harcourt of Harcourt Brace Jovanovich Publishing. I'd occasionally meet Steven after a race at the St. Francis Yacht Club across from Presidio Park in San Francisco proper. This yacht club was for the well-to-do. There was a "Men's Bar" where women were not allowed. There were other bars and rooms going left, right, up and down. The employees were mostly Filipinos and these people I delighted in. They were kind to me and even though I often forgot to bring any money they would bring me drinks and show me the upstairs, downstairs, and the workings of the kitchen. It was an active time with fifty boats and their crews filling the yacht club after each section of the race. The boat my boyfriend was crewing on won the series. There were parties I was included in. At the celebration dinner I was seated next to Hastings Harcourt and throughout the evening my friends, the waiters, brought me free drink coupons.

To get *Bohemia* home from San Francisco Mom entered the Cal Coastal Race. I was on a crew and assigned "dishwasher." When it came to washing up the dinner dishes, Mother said I could use one teapot of water.

I sarcastically asked, "Can I heat it?"

Mother said, "Half the pot."

That made for an even bigger challenge to get eight plates, glasses, tableware and pots and pans clean each night.

There were two crews consisting of four people each who worked a 4-hour watch. A watch consists of 4 hours when you are on deck, awake, sailing the ship, and trying to make the boat go as fast as it can by changing the sails often for optimum speed. That is the easy part. After 4 hours of watch you kick the opposite watch member out of your berth and get your 4 hours of sleep. This doesn't sound so bad until you realize watches get broken down in this schedule 8 a.m. to noon you are on deck, noon to 4 p.m. you are off, 4 p.m. to 8 p.m. you are on, 8 p.m. to midnight you are off and can usually sleep. Midnight to 4 a.m. you are on . . . awake . . . responsible. This is the torture watch. Fine the first night (hey, I'm strong), but a real killer by the fifth day of this continual rotation, 4 a.m. to 8 a.m. sleep, lovely sleep, precious sleep, then 8 a.m. to noon almost easy . . . And so it goes day after day.

One night I heard my brother Jim being woken for his watch and telling the just off watch crew, "I'll pay you, you name the price, anything, just let me sleep."

It didn't work. He had to stand watch. We made it to Los Angeles after five days of constant sailing. We didn't win the race, but the boat didn't sink either. And that night it was so nice to crawl into a real bed and get a full night's sleep.

Whistle Wing V needed to be taken to Santa Barbara where Hastings Harcourt lived. I travelled on her up the coast of California with Steven. *Whistle Wing V* was a large, silver-colored racing boat. It was rigged for fast sail changes. It had flat topsides. Only wenches, halyards, and the tiller penetrated the otherwise flat surface. We were motoring through the Channel Islands, owned by the military, when a Coast Guard boat appeared at our stern.

Through the captain's bullhorn we heard, "You are in military waters. You must vacate the area. We are practicing maneuvers and your boat looks like a good target. Vacate the area immediately."

Glad to know our military was watching out for our best interests.

The Santa Barbara Yacht Club doesn't have many slips. When more boats than slips occur, the practice is to put bumpers on the side of your boat and tie up to the boat already tied to the dock. This chain can go ten boats deep. To get to shore you have to step over all the other boats closer to the dock. In the daylight this isn't much of a problem. At night, after a few of the free alcoholic beverages, getting back to your berth is an adventure. The boat decks are wet with dew. The boats bop up and down with the ocean swells. There aren't good handholds and it is dark. I didn't fall in, but swimming might have been easier.

After the sailing success *Whistle Wing V* had in San Francisco, Hastings decided to take the boat to Florida for its prestigious sailboat series. Steven was asked to crew from Santa Barbara through the Panama Canal to Florida. He invited me to join him. I had to weigh the question: An all-expense-paid six-month adventure following the coast of Mexico, through the Panama Canal to Florida or starting college? Well, college could wait.

The first leg of the trip involved a race from Los Angeles to Mazatlan. Women were rarely invited to be part of a racing crew. Steven raced and I was flown to Mazatlan in Hastings' private airplane. Entering the city was an experience in world commerce. A private U.S. plane didn't just land and breeze in past security. There were inspectors and these inspectors weren't so concerned with whatever you were bringing in as much as the amount you would pay them to bring it in. Now that wasn't the tricky part. The tricky part was these first inspectors had bosses who would come out as soon as the first payments were received to make sure all was on the up and up and to say "those items aren't allowed in the country" unless ... The second rung of inspectors were then paid, and more than the first inspectors because they held a higher rank. This continued through four different ranks of officers before all was cleared.

Mazatlan has a lovely crescent beach, a large harbor, and is full of history. It is also a tourist town.

Sitting on the beach it isn't long before a young Mexican boy asks, "You would like to buy this beautiful turquoise ring, no?"

What I hadn't counted on was Steven becoming extremely possessive. I was no longer able to take a walk by myself or swim when the mood struck without him insisting on escorting me. I'd always been allowed to go where I wanted when I wanted—long walks by myself. That was how I kept my sanity. It soon became apparent this was not going to work. I needed my independence. I had to part ways and head back to the States. I flew home on a commercial airplane.

Mother had moved from our condo in Del Mar to an apartment called the Rondelet across from the San Diego Yacht Club. Here I stayed while I figured out my next move. It was almost Christmas when the doorbell rang. It was my brother Jeff. He had walked the four miles from the airport home. He'd also been crewing a boat to Florida and had decided to leave when they reached the Panama Canal. He could have called to say he was coming home and that he needed a ride from the airport. He didn't. He wanted to surprise us.

It was Jeff's year for the TR3. He commuted back to Del Mar for his last semester of high school.

Mother's apartment complex didn't like teenagers. I'd sleep some nights at the yacht club on *Bohemia*. One afternoon at the yacht club I was paged to the office. A police officer was there. The policemen said he'd been told I stole the rug from the lobby of the Rondelet. I was very confused. I'd never cheated or stolen anything in my life. Management said they saw me in the lobby. Duh. The complex is locked and the only way to Mother's apartment was through the lobby. Where on the boat could I hide a 6' x 8' rug? As if a rug is exactly what every boat needs. Mother had quite the talk with Apartment Management, who decided *It must have been some other teenager.*

§

CHAPTER 20

Ten Flights of Stairs

I learned I could attend the University of California at San Diego as a non-enrolled student. The only difference was I had to ask the professor to sign a form allowing me to take his class. I could live on campus. I had a room on the tenth floor of a dorm with a view of the ocean. It was a room meant for three students, but I had only one roommate. I became obsessive about only taking the stairs. Ten flights of stairs three times a day was all the exercise I needed to stay thin.

I'd talk to lots of students on a bench outside my dorm. One young man was about to depart for a year to work on a kibbutz in Israel. I wished him well. Three months later, I received a brown paper package tied only with string. Inside was a dress he'd sent me. It was caftan style in coarse muslin dyed in earth tones. I found it amazing the package reached me intact and he was inspired to send it.

I considered myself an honest person and thought I had never lied growing up. I was wrong. I was told to lie at the nursing home about my age when visiting Father. When I was shown how easy it was to change my birth date on my California Driver's License, I began a new lie. Doctoring the license required a sharp pencil and a good eraser. Erase a few edges on that number 8 in my birthday 1958. Take the pencil and reinforce a line and a curve to make a 5 and, voila, 1955, three years older and over twenty-one, the drinking age in most states. I was good to go out dancing all night.

I liked to hike from my dorm to the beach. The closest beach was Black's Beach down a little known road. This was one of the few Californian beaches where nude sunbathing was allowed, although I did not partake. The nude beach also attracted lots of sailors on leave. Sailors were best avoided. There was only one house on this strand of beach called "the mushroom house." I knew the house sitter and would ring the doorbell to see if he was home. The actual house was four stories above the beach with an elevator on the sand to take visitors up. If he wasn't home I'd continue my hike over the many rocks until I reached Scripp's Pier and La Jolla Shores Beach, a lovely cove great for swimming and surfing.

I took a Polynesian Culture class to learn more about the South Seas. I was still hoping to one day make it to Tahiti. The final in this class included a luau with a pig roasted in the ground. I had to learn and perform a Tahitian dance. Again, I was embarrassed to be on stage but found I could hide behind other dancers who seemed to know what they were doing.

The Wilderness class I took studied eco-systems. This course included overnight back-packing trips. One hike was in the snow. My brother's old Boy Scout boots fit my feet and were great for hiking. I brought a hard-boiled egg and water. I didn't know to pack a sleeping pad. Trying to sleep on snow covered ground was impossible. Fortunately, the professor, Mike, a graduate student, willingly shared his pad with me. A four-day backpacking trip in the Mammoth Mountains was the final in this course. At night I kept imagining a bear outside and would continually hit the sides of my tent to "scare the bear away." I didn't get much sleep. I think I'd seen Disney's *The Parent Trap* too many times.

After Jeff graduated from high school, Mother moved to Boulder City, Nevada. Mom's yacht club friends wanted to throw her a going-away party, and a full evening was planned. Part one included a sail on *Bohemia*. Part two was food and drink at a friend's house. Lisa and I drove to the Yacht Club together. I was a Junior Member and we were waved through security. Upon getting onto the boat Lisa slipped on the damp wood deck and promptly dislocated her knee, again. I needed to get her to an emergency room. Her father had worked at the Pentagon so a military hospital would be free. Downtown San Diego had one of the best and there we headed. A few hours later Lisa emerged on crutches. We caught up with Mom's party and found everyone in good spirits. And for a second time I had to deliver Lisa home on crutches.

I was considering transferring to Colorado College. Ron, who'd crewed on *Atorrante*, was studying psychology at the University of Colorado, Boulder. He said he had a friend at Colorado College and if I flew to Denver he'd drive me to Colorado Springs. It was a three-hour drive south and we set out early in the morning. It started to snow. We kept going but soon found ourselves sliding into a snowdrift at the side of the freeway. Have I mentioned I really don't like cold? It took an hour to free the car and continue. We met his friend and were taken on a tour of the campus. The college had a very collegiate feel with the old stone buildings and the newly fallen snow. His friend's dorm was an old Victorian building. On the fourth floor was a line of little doors, 3' high by 18" wide. I opened one. There was nothing inside. I imagined these were where the little people lived. I think it was these doors that persuaded me to apply to Colorado College. It definitely wasn't the weather.

§

Chapter 21

Sandals in the Snow

I was accepted to Colorado College. I felt a sense of history just entering its halls. This college is known for its block system where one class is taken at a time for a month and then a new subject chosen. This worked very well for theatre and art courses, but not as well for history or math. Often we were told to go home and read a book to be discussed the next day—great, Machiavelli's *The Prince* in one night. I was fresh from California and seriously thought two pairs of socks with my sandals would keep me warm through the new fallen snow. After a year and a half I never did learn to dress for the cold.

I lobbied for and was given a single dorm room. I took photos from old sailing calendars and pasted the pictures to the ceiling. I now had the ocean above me to ease me to sleep. On the dresser I placed a glass unicorn my brother John had given me. It lost its horn when a dorm mate and I were playing beach ball volleyball in my room—collateral damage. I taped photos of my family to the wall. One evening I looked over and realized that all the photos were in color except the one of Father which was black and white. The unintentional symbolism hit hard.

This college encouraged professors to invite their students to their homes for a dinner or reception. The first college course I took was actually three blocks (months) to study Renaissance culture: The art, history, philosophy, music, and religion—a complete overview. There were three professors and we were invited to one of their houses for a "get to know you" social. We were told the punch was "spiked," but not *how* spiked. I found myself in a rather embarrassing situation being tipsy and sitting on the curb in front of this turn-of-the-century home. One of my professors, Kenneth Burton, who was also the school's chaplain, came out and sat down on the curb next to me.

He inquired, "Do you need help getting back to your dorm? Is there anything I can do to help?"

"No, I'd simply had a little too much punch," I explained.

He answered, "Moderation, my dear child, everything in moderation."

Colorado Springs sits at the foot of Pike's Peak. I borrowed a friend's bike and would bike to the Garden of the Gods. In fall the aspen trees turn these magical colors and flutter in the breeze looking like a sea of butterflies. Hiking Pike's Peak was one of the few times I felt trading my ocean for aspens for a year was worth it.

One long weekend four female students and I set off to ski in Aspen. We didn't realize until we arrived there late at night that a John Denver ski event was happening and there was not a hotel room to be had. We begged, we pleaded, we said we'd sleep in the corridor, in a closet, any space, but the answers were no. What does a group of smart CC coeds do? We decide we will hit the disco with our fake IDs and find someone there who'd put us up for the night. We pranced into this dark dance bar and started asking every guy we danced with, could we go home with them? Being innocent and naïve young women we at least also insisted that all five of us needed to stay together. In the end, we had no takers for five, and ended up at 3 a.m. at the all-night bagel shop. The next day, full of renewed vim and vigor, too much coffee, and not enough sleep, we started changing clothes in the middle of the street, as snow was falling around us.

A car stopped and asked, "What are you girls doing?"

It was an old friend of Tracy's. She'd tried calling him the night before on the slim chance he had a sofa big enough for five. Indeed, he did. The next two nights we stayed at his condo. In the meantime, Patty realized she had lost her purse. Where could it be? She couldn't/ wouldn't/shouldn't have left it in the disco the night before! Ahhh, but she had. Five young eighteen-year-olds walked into the Aspen police station, heads held high, to ask if anyone had turned in a purse. Yes. Someone from the disco did? Amazing. The police didn't put two and two together of what eighteen-year-olds were doing in the disco at 2 a.m. or maybe they did and that is why Aspen is so popular.

The next term I took French. I have a hard time with foreign languages. I just don't hear the subtle differences in pronunciation. I was great at the written part. I can learn anything I see in writing, but orally I'm at a loss. This course was 3 hours in the morning and then 3 hours in a sound lab in the afternoons. It was agony. Halfway through the month I got laryngitis. This was a gift from heaven. The French professor would call on me and as I whispered the answer back all pronunciation issues were too soft to be heard. I wasn't up for the second month of this class and postponed it.

In college I wanted to attempt some of the things that when growing up my brothers had told me time and time again I couldn't do. Singing was one of the activities I had been mercilessly teased about. I joined the college choir hoping I would improve my skills. The piece we were to sing was in Latin. I had no idea how to pronounce the words nor did I know how to sight read the notes. I tried to listen to those next to me to keep pace with where to look on the paper in front of me, but was totally lost. When it came time for the performance, I did an excellent job of mouthing the song and saving the real performers from any disgrace my singing out loud would surely have caused.

I also took ballet in college because I wasn't very good as a child and felt I might tone some muscles and learn a little coordination. I liked the warm-ups at the bar. Easy, not too technical and didn't expose my two left feet. There was a live pianist and an older, gentle, gay male instructor. The floor exercises totally embarrassed me and I tried to slip out of class before revealing my clumsy, self-conscious true dancing ability. There were two experienced male dancers in the class who came simply to stay in shape. One was tall, freckled with red hair and shy. The other was dark-haired and the son of a minister. Both were named David. One night I received a phone message that David had called to ask me out dancing. There was a large fancy hotel at the top of the hill called the Broadmoor with a dance floor that he wanted to take me to.

I called back leaving a message, "Sure, I would love to."

I didn't know which David was going to show up, but I had a favorite dance dress I liked to wear. It was deep burgundy and wrapped around with a flowing hemline. It was David, son of the minister, who knocked on my door that evening. I had a nice glass of chardonnay and spent a few hours on the dance floor.

When I excused myself to go to the ladies' room, a woman there asked, "How many years have you two been dancing?"

I replied, "About two hours now."

It is nice to have a partner who knew what he was doing even if I had an innate urge to try and lead from my elementary school days. When I returned back from dancing, there was a note on my dorm door that an old boyfriend from San Diego had flown his private plane to Colorado Springs to see me. Well, I guess I'll have to go find him. I did at a fraternity house. I found he was a little worse for wear from their generous alcohol hospitality.

I remarked, "Maybe it is best if we meet in the morning for breakfast," and left. We did go out for breakfast, but there were no "sparks" flying.

When I flew home for Christmas, my brother Jim met me at the airport. I didn't recognize him. He'd completely shaved his head and was wearing army fatigues. I walked by him three times. I'm sure he was laughing up a storm to himself. When he finally decided to speak, I still had to look twice.

I exclaimed, "What is this new look?"

He nonchalantly replied, "I've a part in a Beckett play and needed to shave my head."

I guess if you are going to that extreme for a part in a play you might as well have a laugh at your sister as well.

The musical *Cabaret* was scheduled for production back in Colorado. If I took the theatre class that block I could work on the production. The set and lighting professor was Dick, and his wife, Polly, was the costume instructor. It was a delightful month of going to the theatre everyday without anything else on my plate. The course included set design, sewing costumes, and working backstage during performances—no acting! Father had a large collection of records from musicals that he'd played often and *Cabaret* had been one of my favorites. The cast party was a bit of a distance from the college and I rode my bike to it. When I left the party, it was quite dark and I learned what the term "black ice" meant. The wheels of my bike went straight out from under me. I survived with only skinned knees and elbows and learned a great respect for Colorado winter nights.

My professor Dick asked if I would like to earn some money running sound for the Utah Ballet Company that was scheduled to perform.

"Great," I responded, without hesitation.

The night of the performance Dick showed me how to turn on the reel-to-reel tape and where the sound switch and volume controls were. He left the booth to work backstage. The curtains opened and I got the cue in my headset to start the sound. The tape was going, but there was no sound. Where was that audio switch? Is this the volume control? Was there a mute button I needed to push? The dancers were poised, ready to start. Adrenalin was kicking in, but the sound wasn't. Dick was running up to the booth as the curtains on stage started to close. Here, I thought I liked to play with buttons. He calmly showed me again the sequence and returned backstage. The curtains opened a second time. The reel-to-reel was rolling and fortunately there was sound. He did not hire me to run sound again.

I'd always wanted to go white water rafting. It sounded similar to body surfing but not as wet. I signed up for a "White Water Weekend." But this was Colorado. It snowed. Instead of cancelling the trip, the outfitter offered an exchange for a horse trail ride through the Colorado wilderness. Having grown up wanting a pony I signed up. We stayed in a rustic old lodge. Notice the words "rustic" and "old"—which really meant cold, no insulation and the heat source being the wood stove. They offered the option of sleeping in a "converted chicken coop." The romantic in me thought how many times in life is one able to say they slept in a chicken coop. Hey, I was from California, and clueless. That is what I chose. What is even colder than a rustic lodge? A converted chicken coop covered in snow. I froze. What was I thinking? I arose to the smell of coffee and bacon. Too bad I was vegetarian—that bacon smelled really good. I'd had some experience with horses: A summer horse camp, begging my babysitter Sue to take me riding, and Janice's horse. They saddled the horses and off we went. I loved to gallop although most trail rides don't give the rider much opportunity for this. Halfway through this beautiful wooded terrain we came upon a wild horse. I didn't think these really existed. I thought they were made up for the benefit of princes in fairy tales. The trail leader said we were actually in great danger.

From a wild horse? I thought.

The guide explained, "Wild horses love any fillies that cross their paths and become quite aggressive in a desire to mate."

Ahhh, just like some sailors I'd met. This time we were encouraged to gallop—fast—back to the stables at the old lodge.

While at Colorado College I did have a crush on a fellow student. He was in the fraternity Sigma Phi across the street from my dorm. His name was Larry and he was very shy. He played the saxophone and I'd go over to the frat house to try and get him to play for me. I'd anonymously leave flowers or fresh strawberries in a number of the lads' mailboxes without a note. If I was up for a card game, I'd walk into the frat and say, "Anyone up for poker?" I'd then talk them into opening up the "bar." We were in a serious game one night when before we knew it the sun was coming up. How did that happen? I had classes to get to. When it came time for the fraternity's annual dance, there was a note that Larry from the fraternity had called. I called back to find out if it was the Larry I had a crush on or the Larry I played poker with who'd asked me to the dance. It was Larry the poker player.

I replied, "Of course, I'd love to go with you."

As most fraternity parties go, I don't remember many details.

§

Chapter 22

Varnishing the Hatch

The summer I was nineteen I lived on *Bohemia* at the San Diego Yacht Club. Technically this isn't allowed but Mother had moved to Nevada and I needed a place to stay. She hired me to sand and varnish the teakwood. Upkeep on wood boats moored in damp salty conditions is constant. I didn't mind sanding. I could get a sense of rhythm and eventually see the wood's exquisite grain and color. The varnishing was more complicated. Varnish is finicky and needs dry weather to set well. Even running varnish through nylon to get out lumps can leave air bubbles that brush on and show. The best way for me to do this right was investigate how the other boat maintenance workers managed. I walked the docks.

I looked for boats with pristine smooth hatches and railings and then if anyone was about I'd ask, "How did you do that?"

I learned slightly overcast with no chance of rain or fog is best. This Mexican worker had the most luxurious varnish job I'd seen. He offered to take a look at what I needed done. We walked over to *Bohemia* and I showed him the prepped hatch.

He stated, "I'll do it for you."

"Really?" I replied, "I can't afford to pay you."

He answered, "Can you buy me lunch?"

"Of course." There was a handshake to seal the deal.

Mother was very impressed with "my" varnish job.

Since I wasn't suppose to be living on the boat it necessitated getting up early before any personnel that mattered appeared. I had to walk up the dock to the bathrooms to brush my teeth and shower. I'd tip toe back to the boat late at night. Most boats leave a light on to keep the natural occurring mildew at bay. One foggy night I was scared half to death. I saw down the dock a tall and short figure. As I neared them they flapped their wings flying straight at me. When I'd regained my composure, I realized the tall one was a giant egret and shorter one a blue night heron. I named them Harvey and his sidekick Elwood. I wondered what their relationship was and what they talked about strolling the docks at night.

The prestigious sailboat raced called "The America's Cup," is held every four years and Dennis Connor, a member of the San Diego Yacht Club, had been the skipper that won the cup for the US against foreign competitors in the last match. Although the race would be held in Newport, Rhode Island, Dennis spent summers with a crew honing their skills. The boat they used was docked three slips down from ours. These serious sailors would walk by daily with rarely a smile on their faces. They were taking this sport far too seriously. I could usually get a young man to stop and chat for a bit but not this lot. Years later when I returned to the Yacht Club with my fiancé I had the pleasure of introducing him to Dennis Connor who was having lunch on the Yacht Club deck. My fiancé had hair to the middle of his back and could have been labeled "hippie." I like the juxtaposition of this world-renowned yachtsman shaking hands with my Oregon long hair.

During that summer I took the opportunity to drive to Burbank to visit Father's old boss O.B. Johnston. O.B. took me to lunch.

I asked him, "If I wanted to work for Disney what courses should I take in college?"

He was very patient with me and set up a meeting with Disney Studios personnel to answer my questions.

He then said, "I'll set up a meeting for you with Disney's CEO, Card Walker, as well if you'd like to meet him."

Astonished, I replied, "I don't need that second meeting at this time, but I greatly appreciate your offer, maybe after I graduate college."

I also visited my old elementary school. The same principal was still there. She gave her condolences about Father and said she wished she could hand me back all the absent excuse letters he'd written over the years. The teachers and staff would always pass them around loving Father's sense of humor.

§

Chapter 23

Art in the Greatest Art City
in the World

For the second term of my sophomore year at Colorado College I enrolled in a Study Abroad program. It was the beginning of 1979 and I was headed to Europe to study art in one of the greatest art cities in the world, Florence, and theatre in London. The program was two months in each city starting with Florence. I slept in a modest room provided by an Italian woman who told me to call her Senora. She lived in a rather generic apartment complex outside of the historical part of Florence. Getting off the bus I often had a problem remembering which apartment was hers. Senora had a brother who shared her bedroom and worked nights and slept days while she worked days and slept nights. She would leave bread, jam and dark coffee on the table for breakfast. She would have already left for work as a miniature portrait painter.

Dinner was four courses, more than I could ever manage to eat. First there was soup, and then pasta with a light red sauce. After that the entree of fish, chicken or eggs was served. Last was the cheese and fruit plate with espresso. In the center of the table was a light red wine in a bottle with a rooster on it. Very important, she would tell me in Italian, that the wine bottle had a rooster on its label. One night Senora served a fish with a bone in the middle. I've a fear of snakes and eels and will leave this in the realm of *I really don't want to know what meat she just served m*e, as I poured myself another glass of the Chianti.

The shower in this apartment confused me. There was a spigot where water could come out but it was in the middle of the room. If I were to turn it on water would get all over the bathroom.

I asked Senora about this and she said, "Yes, you use the water and then you use the mop."

I did see a drain also in the middle of the floor. I guess this was one way to keep the whole bathroom thoroughly cleaned on a regular basis.

My days were spent exploring this city where art, famous art, awe-inspiring art, was literally around every corner. When the official class lectures were finished, I liked best to aimlessly wander the streets. Each alleyway or road had its own personality, its own history, its little businesses that were hidden under sliding doors. Every day the street would change character as one sliding door would open and another would close leaving me wondering, *is this the right street?*

It was winter, even though it was rainy, tourists still swarmed the famous sites. As a student I had free entrance to the Uffizi Museum where I sat in front of Botticelli's, "The Birth of Venus," for hours. An Italian artist saw me and invited me to join him and a group of friends for a day in the country and a sketching session at his home 20 minutes up the road by train. I went. It was beautiful countryside and the modeling was harder than I'd imagined. I had to stay in the same position for hours. Today, I wonder if somewhere in Florence there is a painting that bears a slight resemblance to me. He took the group of us to lunch at a little bistro in his small village.

Other days I'd take a bus, any bus, and ride it until it ended in the hills on some piazza. I'd ask the bus driver when the bus was headed back to the city and then go explore. In the little plaza sat a fountain and in front of the stores were men in chairs who would eye me up and down as an intruder. I saw a dirt road and headed up it. There were olive trees on both sides with sheep and chickens running loose under them. I passed cottage houses with clothes drying in the sun. I felt both enthralled with this countryside and embarrassed that I might be intruding on someone's private life. But the sun was shining: The smells and sounds were mesmerizing.

I had a hard time resisting three foods in Italy: First were the pastries. These would be displayed in café windows on every street. The shells were light and flaky with smooth cream fillings. Then there was gelato. One student would report the best gelato stand is next to the Ponte Vecchio, another would say a few blocks from the Pitti Palace. It wouldn't be right to name my own favorite until I'd tried all locations mentioned. Last was a family restaurant a friend and I stumbled upon. It was next to the open market. It had long tables for family dinners and café-style ordering at the register. I couldn't read the menu. The owner led me into the kitchen and said point to the dish I wanted. The aromas were amazing and I chose this chicken that had braised all day in a mixture of garlic, onions, and mushrooms. One of the best meals I've ever eaten.

There was this grand building isolated up on a hill not far from Florence that was a curiosity. My girlfriend Cindy and I heard there was a bus that went that way and we set aside a Saturday to explore. It was an old monastery, The Basilica di San Miniato al Monte, still in use and full of brown-clothed monks.

We didn't want to trespass, but when a large, dark-skinned monk opened the door to the monastery and asked, "Would you like a tour?," it seemed rude not to. He took us both by the hand and led us into the sanctuary. He was telling us the story of this monastery, although our Italian wasn't catching most of it, we were going by feel. He kept leading us down staircases into lower and lower chambers. It is an interesting juxtaposition of trusting one leading you by the hand in a Holy place and the natural fear of the unknown. I kept thinking *where was he taking us?* We took steps down into deeper and darker crypts. An hour later we emerged into the daylight again and thanked him as best we could. To make money the monastery made and sold Anise liqueurs. We felt an obligation to buy a few. By taste I hoped they had other sources of revenue.

We'd heard the town of Fiesole up the hill had excellent pizza. A bus went that direction and we were on it. This town overlooked Florence. We could eat from the deck and see Giotto's Campanile (bell tower), Brunelleschi's dome, and the Basilica di Santa Croce. The pizza was light, thin crusted and similar to a baked flour tortilla, very crunchy, with lots of attention given to the lightly marinated vegetables on top.

Young Italian men hiss instead of whistle. It made me feel I was surrounded by snakes. I began to actually miss the sailors in San Diego who'd hoot and holler when I drove by them in the TR3 on my way to the yacht club.

With the university we spent a week in Rome. The Roman ruins sitting next to the new buildings absolutely transfixed me. To wander amongst these ancient columns was a privilege. We had the opportunity to go underground into the catacombs where the bones of the Christians were buried in the walls. It was astounding to me that these people believed in their religion so strongly that they chose to live their life underground.

I even had the cliché experience of spending an evening in front of the Trevi Fountain. There were some Italians there performing music. Then a few asked me to dance and for a moment I felt I was part of an Audrey Hepburn movie.

Cindy and I took a very crowded bus, barely room to breathe, to the docks at Naples where we caught a boat to the Island of Capri. We were enchanted. The town center was on a steep hill above the harbor. It was off-season and most of the pensions were closed.

We found one hotel clerk who said, "We are painting the rooms, but you can stay here for half price if you would like."

"Very much so," I responded.

We wandered back to the center of the village where an elderly man with a cane insisted, "I will be your escort around my island."

He led us along an old path that encircled the rim. There were breathtaking views of the Mediterranean Sea around every bend. Near the end of the trail he invited us to his home. He gave us each a glass of wine. I think he would have liked us to have stayed for hours, but as soon as we could politely take our leave we did.

Back in Rome we visited the Vatican museum and glimpsed the impossible ceilings of Michelangelo. That didn't move me as much as walking into the Church of St. Peter's where I was tiptoeing as quietly as possible because a church service was in process in the main chapel. I slipped into a little alcove and was awestruck by a sculpture. I wasn't looking for it. I just happened upon it. It was the "Pieta." Mary with Jesus sprawled on her lap done by Michelangelo. I stared and stared. I had no idea art could be this emotionally moving.

On a Saturday I took the train to Venice. It was pouring rain, but was warm in the train looking out at the countryside. Once in Venice a canal boat took me down to the St. Mark's Square where as a child Father had sponsored the "Kick a Pigeon" poster contest. On this day, twelve years later, the Cathedral of St. Mark felt cold and damp. I thought maybe lunch would warm me up. I took a canal boat back upstream and wandered the narrow streets, over little bridges, until I came to a restaurant that fit my budget. Three-course meal with special from the sea and wine for three dollars. The men looked at me as I entered and sat at a table alone. I was later told that it isn't proper for a single woman to dine by herself. The soup and wine warmed me and the seafood special seemed particularly good until I made the mistake of looking closely and recognized tentacles on those long pieces of fish. I would never have tried it if it hadn't been written in Italian. I caught the afternoon train back to Senora who was appalled at how wet I was and sent me straight to bed with a cup of broth. It did feel good to be in a warm bed.

Senora threw me a going-away banquet and invited her brother and neighbors. She made a soufflé and my favorite dessert, Floating Clouds: Soft vanilla custard with meringue. My Italian still wasn't the best and the men at the table were laughing uproariously at something said.

Senora translated for me, "They said what small breasts you have."

Senora really knew quite a lot of English, she just never let on. She wanted to make sure I learned Italian.

§

Chapter 24

Nice is Nice

The study abroad program was eight weeks in Florence and eight weeks in London. There was a week in between where we could travel to make our way to London. Cindy and I decided on a route through France. We started with a side trip to the Swiss Alps and stayed in the town of Annecy, with a huge lake, and very cold weather. Nice was next. When we arrived, a woman at the train station convinced us to stay at her lodgings. This was really an extra room in a retirement home and we didn't feel comfortable there. At dawn we snuck out and found new lodgings in a nice little hotel.

I have always liked to read the menus on restaurant doors to find the best deal. There was a little restaurant I saw with a three-course meal for around five dollars.

I suggested, "We should eat here tonight."

Cindy agreed. We went walking on the beach promenade while looking for dance clubs we might go dancing. We ate at the little restaurant, but found the clientele a little on the scruffy side.

When our waitress presented me the bill, she whispered in my ear, "I heard a couple of the other patrons saying they were going to rob you when you left."

This is where years of playing football came in handy. We made a plan to walk out calmly, cut left, the opposite direction from our hotel, then a quick right, and run as fast as we could back to our room. We arrived safe and out of breath. We cancelled our plans to go dancing that night. The next day, while again walking on the promenade, Cindy began a conversation with a good-looking French lad.

He asked, "Can a friend and I escort you to dinner and dancing tonight?"

Cindy quickly replied, "Yes!"

When we met up later, the "friend" was a rather older gentleman and "my date." Dinner and dancing wasn't quite what I had pictured, but Cindy had a good time.

The next day we boarded the Mediterranean Coast Train. The train runs on a narrow cliff path with the ocean on the left side and small isolated villages on the right. We got off at a desolate-looking stop. Up the hill was a youth hostel with a view of the ocean. We found it warm and charming. There was an option for dinner as well. It was rabbit stew. If I was ever going to eat rabbit this was the day and it was delicious.

§

Chapter 25

All the World's a Stage

The London course study included: Architecture, history, English politics and theatre. I was pleased that the chaplain from Colorado College, Kenneth Burton, was one of the professors. He'd grown up in London and had attended Cambridge University. Throughout my stay we'd "bet each other pints of beer" over some fact we disagreed on and would "pay up" at the next theatre production we attended. We were fortunate to see plays at the Royal Shakespeare Theatre as well as their Stratford Theatre. We saw many exceptional productions at the Royal National Theatre and Vanessa Redgrave in a production of Ibsen's *The Lady from the Sea*. The production I liked best was a Royal Shakespeare Theatre presentation of Shakespeare's *Taming of the Shrew*.

The curtain went up and an actor on a motorcycle drove on to the stage yelling, "Fire, Fire!"

I've seen a lot of theatre, but I was ready to exit the theatre as soon as the others moved so I wouldn't get crushed in a mob. But no one moved. It was actually part of the play. He'd ridden into Katherine's bathroom where she was taking a bath. I'd been fooled, but it truly set the stage for all the conflict that follows.

The day before my twenty-first birthday our college group toured Cambridge University and slept in their dorms. I loved the feel of this old collegiate town and decided to stay an extra day instead of heading back to my London accommodations. I found a Bed and Breakfast where I left my backpack and went to breathe in the town on my own. The old buildings, the cobble streets in the city centre were all enthralling. Each of Cambridge's different colleges had a unique quality and definitely a far superior dress code than California campuses. I sat by the river and wondered how "punting" had become a sport. Maybe it was one of those activities that began out of necessity, getting goods to the market before they spoiled, while now moving a boat with a long pole frankly looked silly.

Chinese food sounded good to me for dinner, and I found a little restaurant not far from the campus. It wasn't long after I was seated when a young man sat down in the chair across the table.

He inquired, "Didn't I see you in Paris last week?"

Ironically, I had been in Paris, but it was *two* weeks ago.

"Not last week," I replied.

I did think it was a rather clever introduction. He stayed and we shared dinner. He then suggested we venture to one of Cambridge's prestigious pubs for a birthday pint. There is a mystique about those carved wood walls and high ceilings that take me back in time. We talked and talked even after the pub had closed. He walked me back to my Bed and Breakfast and promised if he were in London in the near future to take me to the Royal Ballet. I hoped he would. There was a parting kiss as I tiptoed up the creaky staircase hoping I hadn't added another notch to the reputation of American girls traveling abroad, although I probably had. I felt a little embarrassed at breakfast not by my actions but by the late hour I'd gotten in.

I caught the train to London and at the reception desk were messages: Mother had called, flowers from an old boyfriend, and a note from my grandmother Eleanor that she was having a friend take me to lunch at Claridges. I really could have used the money instead, although I must say lunch at Claridges was delicious. We had sherry in the foyer where a harpist performed. In the elegant dining room we were served exceptional cuisine and the sherry truffle for dessert was amazing. I would never have treated myself to such a lavish and expensive lunch.

I got tired of trying to untangle my hair everyday so decided to cut it short. Sassoon offered free haircuts at their beauty school. I made an appointment. I came out in tears. I hated the short hair. I hid it under a scarf for a week before I realized maybe a different hairdresser could fix it. I found one downtown next to the Royal Shakespeare Theatre. This hairdresser gave me bangs and added some styling, almost back to the pixie cut of my childhood. I liked it much better.

There was a young man from Boston who frequented the pub closest to our hotel. He'd flirt and ask me out to dinner. After one date I saw him chatting up my girlfriend Cindy. I thought what a cad and took my pint of beer and swiftly but accurately poured it on his head and walked out. Make note: Avoid that pub for the immediate future.

Cindy and I were invited to attend a football (soccer) game. The football club was a bit outside of London and required both a tube and train ride. I found the institution of this sport interesting. This club had its own field and clubhouse, almost like how a country club is set up in our country. Members had privileges and invited guests were welcome. We enjoyed the intensity of the game and the camaraderie afterwards. We had to rush to catch the midnight train back to London. When we arrived at Hyde Park Station, we realized there were some rather drunk and unruly locals trying to chat us up. We felt that this was not the safest situation for two young women to walk the half-mile to our lodgings in Edgeware. We quickly popped into the Hilton Hotel lobby. We decided now was the time to splurge on a taxi.

I couldn't wander London as I did Florence. The town was too big and there were dangerous areas. I did go by Buckingham Palace. I happened to walk by the Rubens, the hotel we'd stayed at as children. There was a doorman out front. I peered into the lobby. I was wearing jeans and a daypack. This hotel was definitely two social classes above my current economic station. I walked on. I was happy I could say I'd once been in that world, and at the same time felt comfortable in the world I now occupied, the student on a shoestring budget.

London did have great public transportation and the trains offered cheap day passes to nearby towns. I took a train to the town of Bath. I found its history fascinating with the Roman baths and world-famous Cathedral. After a walking tour of the historic sites, a new acquaintance said I needed to taste the local stout. I was not a big Guinness fan but I went with him. This stout was exquisite. The best beer I'd ever tasted. I found myself in a dilemma. The last train to London was leaving soon. Do I stay? That meant finding accommodations. I caught the train.

For another day trip I headed to the Isle of Wight. Every summer there is a popular sailboat race out of Cowes. If I found a job here for the summer I could see my sailing friends. There was a job board and I looked for summer positions. One small hotel needed a chambermaid and I went to talk to the owner.

She said, "I will hire you if you can get a work permit."

That should be easy. Students are given work permits. I went to the London Agency in charge of permits and confidently filled out the form. I stood in queue and handed the official my application. It came back stamped "Denied." What?

I asked him, "Why?"

"We already have too many unemployed Brits," he replied.

Right. Okay. Makes sense. Scratch that plan.

Cindy and I went to a matinee of the musical *Chicago*.

The lad behind us in line said, "I want a seat next to them."

We chatted a bit before the play and I thought nothing of it. After the show he invited us to join him for a pint in the pub across the street. Cindy declined but I accepted, and spent the afternoon talking to him. His name was Jason and he was studying at the London School of Economics. He was Afrikaans and said he had a fiancée back in South Africa. I thought great, a new friend. He invited me to a party at his flat a week later and I went. After a bit I heard live guitar playing upstairs and headed there to listen. Jason found me an hour later and wasn't pleased I was listening to the musician and not hanging out with him. I thought, *What about the fiancée back home?*

The London school term ended and Jason invited me to Manchester to visit a mate and go to the horse races.

I love horse races and said, "Yes."

I left most of my luggage at his flat and took only my daypack. We were staying at an apartment rented by an oil rigger who was gone at the time. It was the shabbiest place I've ever entered with a rusty bathtub in the center of the living room. I steadied myself for whatever this weekend would bring. We visited another lad who had invited some friends over to watch a football game on the tellie. With all the drink I easily surmised that the horse races weren't going to happen.

One lad at the party saw my discomfort and suggested, "Would you like to go for a walk?"

"What an excellent idea," and off we went to explore Manchester.

"I know a back way into the zoo," he said. "Do you want to sneak in?"

"Sure," I responded, as he started climbing a fence and helping me up.

We talked, viewed the animals and had a delightful time. Upon returning to the apartment Jason was dismayed that I'd gone on a walk with someone else. The group decided they were hungry and went out for food and more beer. It was very dark. Jason was very drunk. I had to hold him up. I couldn't remember what the apartment we were staying in looked like and we wandered for an hour looking for it. This was not fun.

At dawn I woke Jason and stated, "I am off."

I was taking the morning train somewhere. He was angry, but I was out the door. Then I remembered my main suitcase was at his flat in London. I'd figure out how to retrieve it later.

I took a train to Wales thinking the ocean could brighten my day. There was a grand castle that I stopped to explore and I had lunch in the coastal town of Caernarfon. I discovered the castle was largely just a shell. It had a nice façade but not much else. The wind came up and it started raining. The castle felt dank. I caught a bus heading south along the Welsh coastline. It didn't take long for Sean to take the seat next to me on the bus.

"I'm headed for Aberystwyth where I am staying with a friend and you should join me."

"I'd love to." Free lodging can't be turned down.

That evening Sean, his friend and I ventured down to the local pub that was known for music sessions in a back room. The musicians gladly gave me a chair and let me be part of their evening even though I couldn't sing or play an instrument. They kept trying to come up with American songs, but I told them to play their Celtic favorites.

At one point I left to use the loo when a woman my age queried, "Didn't you go to Torrey Pines High School?"

"Yes, I did," I answered.

She had been a classmate and was in Wales taking courses at the college up the hill.

"That is very nice, but there are some lads in the back room that I really need to get back to."

I spent that night on the sofa and Sean slept on the floor. In the morning I told Sean that I'd be staying on in Aberystwyth for a few more days, while he took the bus south.

Chapter 26

A Welsh Pub

I explored the town of Aberystwyth by daylight. It was interesting with its ancient stone battalions scattered along the shoreline. In a store window I saw a listing for jobs. A pub in Borth needed a barmaid. I could do that.

What possibly made me think I could just walk into a pub and get a job? Maybe in the back of my mind I had held onto Walt's words: "We keep moving forward, opening new doors, and doing new things, because we're curious and curiosity keeps leading us down new paths."

I called, "Would you interview an American without a work permit?"

"Yes, just catch the next bus," the owner replied.

The bus drove through tall hedges, green fields dotted with sheep on a one-lane road. Borth was 30 minutes from Aberystwyth, on the coast, a little hamlet of 200 people. There was a nice beach and that day the sun shone. It looked beautiful. I thought this could be my home for the next while. The main street had buildings on one side and the ocean on the other. The establishment I was looking for was the Hotel Borth. I entered a dark, yet welcoming, lobby, and met the owner, Mr. Thompson. He was a large jolly fellow who took a liking to my good looks and American accent.

He explained, "You'd be behind the bar from 10 a.m. to 2 p.m. and again from 5 p.m. to 10 p.m. You'll get every other Sunday off. You'll have your own room and any food you can salvage from the kitchen. I pay 50 pounds a week."

I took the job. Not that I'd ever worked in a pub before but the thought of a bed and food available any time made up for the low wages. My room was four flights up in what once would have been the attic. The room was only big enough for a single bed. It had a white slanted roof with a little window and a view of the sea. The bath was down the hall. I was delighted to have a pillow to rest my head on. The thing I didn't know when I landed this job was the sunny day that brought me here never came back during the two months I worked here. Then, again, I didn't have much time to walk on the pebble shore and the Welsh aren't known for their golden tans.

This pub was part of the hotel. There were guests staying in the upstairs rooms. There was a formal dining room with white tablecloths and higher ranked employees. The hired help was a large variety of nationalities. The cook was a fine lad from Scotland who liked to flirt with me. The two maids came from Cornwall and were on the shy side. The dining room servers were from England and a little above talking to an American.

I had a little trouble at first. Pints had to be pulled and there was a knack to it I needed to learn. Most of the customers were Welsh. I was in Wales, wasn't I? They tended to speak in Welsh: A language I didn't know existed. They'd ask for pints of bitters, ale, half & half, stout, lager—types of beer I had to learn fast. They also paid in shillings, duh, but it took me a minute to do the mental conversion to U.S. monies and back to English change.

One custom the locals had was to buy a pint for themselves and say, "And one for you, lass."

Night after night I was bought four or five pints. For the first week I thought it would be impolite not to pull myself one and drink it.

During my second week on the job the Scots cook informed me, "It is allowed to charge the customer for the second pint, pocket the money, and say you'll buy yourself one later."

Good to know, I no longer had to try and drink four pints and crawl up the four flights of stairs to my small bedroom.

My boss often worked the bar with me.

He'd announce with glee, "This is my American and she is available."

Generally I can handle some teasing and flirting but most of these regulars were in their older years and my availability to them was never going to be a reality.

On my Sunday off I took the local train to the next town north.

As I got off, a man across the street shouted, "You are from San Francisco."

Puzzled, I answered, "No, San Diego."

"Oh, the butcher said you were from San Francisco."

With that introduction he said his name was Tom and took it upon himself to give me the local tour. Tom was a retired engineer in his 40s who had moved back home to spend his days in a cottage on the creek. He had a girlfriend who lived the next town over. He took me up and down the main street, about all these little villages had. He gave me a tour of a small facility that was experimenting with solar energy. After a cup of tea and meeting his large German shepherd, I bid him farewell to catch the train back to Borth.

I found the nights in Wales chillier than the clothes I'd packed in my little daypack. I saw this gorgeous hand-knit wool fisherman's cardigan in a store window. I went in to acquire about the cost. It had been hand-knit by a resident of Borth by the name of Mrs. Jones. It was

50 pounds, my whole week's wages. But I was in love with it and bought it. That sweater came to serve me for twenty-five years until its elbows became threadbare.

One of the magic moments working in a pub occurs after hours. Pubs close at 10 p.m. but hotel guests can partake much later. If there were a good group of customers and the possibility of a "Sing Song," Mr. Thompson would have all the pub patrons sign the hotel guest registry. They'd proceed with singing late into the night. This was a country that loved their beer and their song. I didn't mind the overtime hours since listening to the music was superb.

Sundays were always a quiet day. Pubs were not allowed to serve alcohol but they could serve what is called a shandy. This beverage is one-half lager and one-half lemonade.

My regulars would come in, order a shandy, and say, "Easy on the lemonade there, lass."

When I left the job in August, Tom who'd given me a tour of Machynlleth, asked, "Can I give you a driving tour of another part of Wales?"

"Yes, that would be very nice," I responded.

We traveled narrow roads into the inner valleys of Wales where coal mining had been the industry for hundreds of years. I found the terrain and pubs we stopped in dark and dreary. We arrived back in Machynlleth quite late and the last train to London had already left.

Tom suggested, "You are welcome to sleep on the sofa." This really meant share it with his German shepherd.

I did. The next day I was gathering my things to head to London when the phone rang. It was Tom's girlfriend. She'd heard from the next-door neighbor that he'd had a young woman spend the night.

Tom replied, "Yes, there is an American here who had shared the couch with my dog."

He then told me, "She wants to meet you. We are to join her for a pint in her village."

I found myself not heading for London, but in a car headed for Aberdovey, to meet the girlfriend. We met at a pub where we had dinner. When the time approached to go back to Machynlleth, Tom asked a friend of his who was leaving to call back and tell him if there were any police on the road. He didn't want a ticket for drunk driving.

His friend called the pub thirty minutes later, "Indeed, the police are out and he best not drive home."

Now I found myself on the girlfriend's couch. Her three young children keep tiptoeing in to get a glimpse of the American girl asleep on their sofa. The next day I did make it to a train to London where I stayed with Father's friends Barbara and Peter.

Jumping ahead in my story for just a minute I have a poignant conclusion to this adventure. After that summer and two years of college I found myself in Ashland, Oregon, working my first job backstage at the Oregon Shakespeare Festival. I had a steady boyfriend named Brian. Tom from Wales came to Ashland and asked the Festival office where I was working. Tom found me backstage setting stage lights.

He asked, "Can I take you out to dinner?"

I had a date with Brian that night. I called Brian.

Brian replied, "You can't turn down free food. Just come over afterwards."

Tom said, rather demanded, "Wear a dress."

He drove me to one of the fancier restaurants in the valley. He ordered wine, which he sent back, too warm. He ordered another wine that he sent back, wrong odor. He finally compromised on a third bottle. He was rather upset that a few items on the menu were not available. I felt this wasn't quite the "mellow" attitude I was accustomed to.

I ordered the scampi and on my third bite Tom said, "Will you marry me?"

"What?" I stammered spitting out the scampi.

"I want you to marry me. Then move with me to Saudi Arabia and cook."

I calmly responded, "I really don't know you well. I've just finished college and am not ready to even think about getting married. No."

The rest of the evening was awkward.

When he dropped me at my apartment, I quickly drove to Brian's house and begged, "Can I please spend the night? Next three nights? I don't dare go home."

When I did return to London after working in the Welsh pub, I had to find Jason. He was somewhat cordial when he handed my luggage back to me and said, "Maybe I'll see you in the States."

Now . . . I could be hallucinating, and my family would say, of course you are, but when I was in Ashland working the lighting board for a South African play titled *The Island* I could swear I saw Jason in the audience. Using my newly acquired good sense I stayed in that light booth until well after the audience had left and exited through an unused side door.

Back in London I stayed my father's colleague, Peter, and his wife, Barbara, for a few days in Pettswood.

Peter asked, "Did you bring your costume?"

"My costume?" I replied confused.

"Do you like to swim?" he asked.

"Love to."

"Then you'll need a swimming costume."

"Ah, costume, bathing suit. Got it. What Southern California girl doesn't have a bikini with her at all times?"

They had three boys, ages eight through twelve. I was taken in as a long-lost older sister. Every morning at my door was a cup of tea with milk or lemon, my choice. I accompanied the family to the equivalent of a Boy Scouts Jamboree. The next day was swimming. To a large community pool we went. I was left to change into my costume in the ladies' changing room while they went to the men's. I felt a little lost but once I spied them in the pool I happily jumped in. Swimming was my element. It was a delightful afternoon. Later, I joined them in their Sunday tradition where neighbors gathered to sip sherry and talk politics.

§

Chapter 27

Will I Be Kidnapped?

Janice, my friend from Thousand Oaks, was studying abroad for a year in Gottingen, Germany. I took a train to Gottingen to see her. She was busy with finals and suggested I visit her roommate's family in Berlin. Her roommate was happy to take me home with her and to West Berlin we went. Here I was staying with a family I did not know, and I did not speak German. I could smile and eat the food they offered me, which was every time I walked in the door, even though it was often meat. West Berlin people were very thankful to Americans. They explained that after World War II they were an isolated city surrounded by Soviet-controlled East Germany. U.S. planes would fly in bringing very much needed supplies of food and medicine.

I asked for a glass of water and was told, "Only cows drink water." That left me to drink many cups of coffee and glasses of wine.

The year was 1979 and the Berlin Wall had been in place since 1961. I had heard stories from Father's colleagues of those who'd risked their lives to escape from East Berlin to the free West. What inspired me on one cold gray day to visit East Berlin? A museum, called the Pergamon, which held a significant artifact, the Wall of Babylon. I took a train on a Saturday and the train stopped at Checkpoint Charlie, the border station between East and West Berlin. Everyone got off and at the guard station I was asked many questions in German that I did not understand. The guard then asked for my passport, which I gave him. He said I could go into East Berlin, but he kept my passport! I was confused, but couldn't ask what was happening. I've never felt more vulnerable to another culture. I proceeded and tried "not worry about it," although I did. I had to put my faith in my own "Jiminy Cricket" and believe he was looking out for me.

The streets of East Berlin were dark. There was no one else walking about. There were no lights, no restaurants. There was lots of destruction and rubble still left from World War II. Half the buildings sat black and demolished.

I found the museum and was practically the only one there. The Wall of Babylon was inspirational, although I wondered why it was here. It has these beautiful shades of blue tile in intricate designs on rounded arches straight out of a fairy tale. After I left the museum I got lost and followed the river. I ended up outside an army barracks and had East Germans whistling and shouting at me. If the whole city wasn't so dark, and I didn't feel like any minute I was going to be kidnapped and forced to stay there the rest of my life, I might not have minded. When I finally found my way back to Checkpoint Charlie, I wasn't sure what was going to happen. Fortunately, they did have my passport and handed it back. I was relieved. Even though I'd been scared, it was a remarkable experience, especially going as a young woman, vulnerable to the elements, the emotions, and beauty, this war-beaten town had shown me.

§

Chapter 28

I Need a Moment's Rest

I arrived in Paris with three weeks before the date of my return ticket to San Diego. I left most of my clothes and large backpack in a locker at the train station and headed out on foot to see the city.

It wasn't long before an older man approached me and stated, "This really is not the safest part of Paris for a young lady to be walking on her own. I will be your escort. Where are we headed?"

I wasn't headed anywhere, but I now decided the Modern Art Museum would be a good destination.

Once there, this older man declared, "I will join you because I know this museum well."

There went my plan of "ditching" him. Not that his knowledge wouldn't be appreciated, but when I enter a museum I have this routine of sitting in a room and absorbing the atmosphere, the people coming and going, and then the art as it sits and what it says after long contemplation. This is a technique hard to explain in French to a stranger.

After his tour he asserted, "You must be hungry, let me take you to the little bistro that all the famous artists frequented. They have a house special merveilleux."

The path of least resistance was to follow and some local history was a good thing. The house special was a Beef Cassoulet and it was delicious.

Now I thought I had my chance to escape, but, no, he exclaimed, "The last thing every visitor to my country has to do is sit at a café with an aperitif and watch the people go by."

Again, I can't say it wasn't delightful, but I did now have a valid escape line: "My hostel locks its doors at 10 p.m. and I really must be going."

I was escorted to the hostel's door and from there I said my goodnight.

New game plan for tomorrow: rise at dawn, slip out the back door and head somewhere, maybe Brittany. That plan I executed flawlessly. On the train I met some girls from Georgia who knew of a great hostel and I joined them.

At the hostel a young man informed me, "You are just in time for the annual Celtic Music Festival and you should join me."

I had only experienced Celtic music once before in the back room of the pub in Wales and I'd enjoyed it tremendously.

Consequentially I responded, "Yes, I would love to."

It was a two-day folk festival, including camping out overnight. I had nothing for such an activity, having left most of my clothes at that train station in Paris. Nor had I prepared, like most of the audience, to bring a picnic or food of any kind. But to lie on the hill on that warm summer night and listen to the live music was mesmerizing. Unlike most times, no one offered me a blanket, piece of bread, or sip of wine. It was still lovely.

There was no train from Brest to Quimper in Brittany and I did not like to back track. I decided to do what Mother always told me never to do—hitchhike. I was covered with dirt from the festival and starving, but put out my thumb. It wasn't long before a car stopped. It was completely packed. There were two Frenchmen in the front and the back was loaded with clothes, food, and fishing equipment.

They said in French, "We'll give you a ride, but you have to sit up front with us."

Now my French wasn't very good, but an adventure was an adventure and I crawled in. They offered me an orange and for those of olden times who were given this precious fruit on Christmas, this orange was a magical gift. I think those two Frenchman truly enjoyed watching me peel and eat that orange.

It was only a 30-minute ride to the first exit in Quimper and I declared, "This is more than generous. Please let me out here."

It was a bit of a walk to the city center, but I wanted to make sure I was going to be let out of the car. I found a bench and started to fall into that exhausted relaxation mode, when a local resident sat down beside me.

"You sure look like you could use some food. Let me take you to my favorite restaurant for lunch," he offered.

I was hungry. He took me to this little café known for its crepes and cider. It was refreshing.

After lunch he suggested, "Come back to my place for some hashish."

I replied, "I don't smoke and I really need to catch a train to Paris, but thank you for a delicious meal."

He walked me to the train station. As I watched him walk up the hill I turned around and headed back into town. I found a little hotel and hoped the rooms wouldn't be too dear.

The woman at the desk took one look at me and stated, "You need a bath."

Duh. The rooms with showers were more than I could afford, but the single was in my price range.

She compromised, "I'll make you a deal. You go wash in the room with the shower and I'll charge you just for the shower then you sleep in the little room."

Yes! I loved the feel of clean water after sleeping on the hard ground. Refreshed, I ventured out to collect a few items for dinner—bread, cheese, and a bottle of beer. Fortunately, I didn't encounter my earlier lunch companion. I had a lovely relaxed evening in my room, and I did catch the morning train back to Paris.

In Paris I needed to find a different hostel for the next few days while I figured out what I was going to do next. I was running low on money and running low on the energy to escape male attention.

An Arab man had come up to me that afternoon and whispered in my ear, "I love you, marry me."

This was getting ridiculous. I decided I'd try to change my plane ticket and return to San Diego a week early. The travel agency could change my flight and I was ready to head home. I returned to the train station to retrieve my backpack. I put the key in the locker. It was empty. What now?

Panicked, I asked the guard, "Where is my luggage?"

"Anything left over three days goes into long-term storage—over there."

"Over there" they did have my backpack and I could even have it back, for a fee.

When I arrived at the airport on my new departure date, I was told my name was not on their list. Okay. They put me on the stand-by list. It was one of those tests of patience that I practiced while sailing. The scheduled plane was going to be delayed a day and all ticketed passengers would get free food and lodging for the night. Did that mean stand-by passengers? I pleaded with the airline to include the stand-by group. They relented and we were soon whisked to a generic airport hotel. The next day as they are calling names to board the plane, mine was the last one called. I made the flight. The plane was late getting into New York and I missed the connecting flight to San Diego. I slept on the airport floor. The next day the airline said the closest they could get me to San Diego was San Francisco. I took the flight and arrived in San Francisco, and then was told the next flight to San Diego would be the following day. I spent that night sleeping on the San Francisco waiting room floor. If you haven't been counting it is taking me four days to get home. When I arrived in San Diego, my brothers weren't home. Jeff was on a sailboat racing to Tahiti. Jim was working a summer theatre festival in Colorado. I called Lisa's brother to give me a ride from the airport to my brothers' apartment. I had to persuade Property Management to give me a key to Jim and Jeff's apartment. After I'd showered, an ex-boyfriend walked into the apartment with his new girlfriend.

I exclaimed, "What are you doing here?"

He responded, "I am house-sitting for your brothers."

Ohhh. At this point I pulled rank and stated, "I am staying here until a brother reappears and I find a place of my own."

He wasn't too happy, but he hadn't been too happy when I broke up with him three years earlier.

My travels through Europe gave me an insight to my needs. I learned my priorities in life started with a warm safe bed. I was most inspired by an honest intelligent conversation. It was respect and sense of humor that I sought in others. My biggest fear was being kidnapped in a communist country. And, I truly missed my family, friends, and ocean.

I did feel a little betrayed when I arrived back in the States, after nine months abroad, that there was no one to say, "Welcome back, how was it? I want to hear your stories."

Mother hadn't exactly disowned her children, but I felt she'd moved on. I did have a bit of the feeling I was an orphan, a Pinocchio that might as well have been swallowed by the whale.

Tuia was the name of the boat Jeff was sailing on. It is approximately a three-week sail from Los Angeles to Papeete, Tahiti. Jeff's job was bowman. A boat could get stuck in the doldrums for days. After twenty-one days at sea, *Tuia* reached Papeete. They took second place by fifteen minutes. Jeff had made it to Tahiti.

Mother also made it to the South Seas. She remarried an old family friend, Sam, who'd been on that original double date with Father back at nursing school. Sam was a dermatologist and had volunteered to spend the summer in American Samoa treating locals for leprosy. Leprosy is a progressive skin disease that with lifetime treatment can be held at bay. Once the local Samoans started getting better they'd stop taking the medication. Sam was there to make sure they had enough of the medicine and that they took it. The compensation for his services was room and board on a tropical beach for three months. Mother loved it.

Another need on the islands was eye care. Mom and Sam collected discarded prescription glasses. They'd take a large box of these for the Samoans to rifle through and take which pair fit their needs. This would literally change their view of the world.

When Sam decided to retire five years later, he and Mother chose to move to the Hawaiian Island of Molokai. Molokai historically is known for its leprosy colony on the Kalaupapa Peninsula. For hundreds of years people with skin disease were rounded up and made to jump ship onto this desolate piece of land. Escape was prohibitive due to high cliffs on one side and a vast ocean on the other. Here the patients would disintegrate far from the sight of human eyes. By the time Sam and Mother moved to Molokai the government had taken control of Kalaupapa and the patients were well supervised and compensated.

§

CHAPTER 29

Behind the Scenes

What I'd missed most during my years in Colorado and my studies abroad was the ocean. I longed for the vast expanse of empty space without houses, roads, stop signs, just a breeze and a horizon full of water. I transferred back to University of California at San Diego. I loved the campus. I loved that I could wear a halter-top and sandals every day of the year. I loved that I could get a tan as I read my biology textbook. Two of my brothers were now UCSD students. I was happy to be home.

My brothers' apartment was a one-bedroom unit a few blocks from campus. In their living room sat Grandmother Helen's Steinway grand piano. It took up most of the living room. I slept under it for a week until I found my own apartment. When my brothers later moved to a rental in Del Mar, I watched the movers harness and lower this piano onto a moving truck. There was a tense time when it hung suspended by the straps they'd wrapped around it. They told my brother this was a very rare Steinway. The Steinway Company had only produced five of this style, called an extended grand, and it was worth a lot of money. This didn't help lessen my anxiety as it swung in the air.

I'd found a listing on a housing board at UCSD: "Roommate wanted to share apartment a block from the beach in Del Mar." This apartment was divided into two large rooms with a door between that could be locked by either side. My half had a bathroom, large living room with a nook to the side that a bed would nicely fit. I had access to Mother's furniture stored in a garage near the yacht club. The other half of the apartment had a kitchen, bathroom and smaller living room/bed area. Its advantage was the kitchen. Since I was anorexic I didn't need a stove and refrigerator. I didn't know my roommate, but there was plenty of privacy and he moved out not long after I moved in. I heard John W. was looking for a place. He'd been studying abroad in Germany with Janice. I had visited him in a hospital in Germany where he was recovering from hepatitis that he'd picked up in Morocco from shellfish. He liked the apartment and we became roommates. He was involved with various political campaigns and would rope me into helping him serve champagne at the fundraisers. These events were held at mansions overlooking the ocean in La Jolla. We'd get to take home any leftover champagne. John had a slight stutter and after a year rooming with him I developed a slight stutter as well. I hadn't known stuttering was contagious.

My apartment was two minutes from my favorite Del Mar beach. I'd cross over the railroad tracks and there I'd be ready to dive head first into the oncoming waves. The water wasn't exactly warm, but it did the trick to wake me up and get ready for a twelve-hour day studying at university.

Sometimes at night I'd go a little bonkers—maybe too much studying, or maybe a hidden desire to be on stage. I'd find my way down to the beach at 10 p.m. There was a restaurant that focused bright lights on the ocean for its clientele. It was there I'd go bodysurfing. I took out my contact lenses so I wouldn't lose them in the ocean. I was swimming blind and literally bodysurfing in the dark. The challenge was relying on instinct. All those years of rafting, a true test of my ability to hear and respond to the swells in the water. It was a thrill. There was the added pleasure of the patrons of the beach side restaurant watching a crazy college student bodysurfing at night. Once when I was waiting for a wave I smelled a distinct marine animal scent. I thought I saw a fin, remember my contact lenses were out, and I truly couldn't see. When the next set of waves came, I confirmed there was a finned creature next to me. Since it wasn't circling, and was actually playing in the waves, I deduced it was a dolphin. I proceeded to try to catch the same waves it did. It caught more. I was delighted to have shared my evening with a dolphin.

Swimming in the ocean, daytime or nighttime, can be dangerous when there is a riptide. A riptide is a strong narrow current that runs perpendicular to the beach. They can quickly pull a swimmer out to sea. As young children we were taught to watch for them. We were told over and over, if ever caught, swim to the side, parallel to the beach, don't try to swim straight to shore. First get free of the riptide and then swim to shore. One late afternoon I was bodysurfing in Del Mar when the next thing I knew a lifeguard was handing me his orange life buoy and instructing me to float while he pulled me to shore. I was peeved. I didn't feel I was in any trouble. He explained I was in a riptide and he needed to get me back to shore. Well. I walked about thirty yards down the beach and dove right back into the water. I wasn't finished swimming yet.

Upon transferring to UCSD I switched from being an English major to a theatre major. In my literature courses professors were interested in dissecting a novel. What did the author intend? In theatre it was a building process. Take the words, use your imagination, and create a world that helps portray the emotions, place, and time. Achieve this through your choice of sets, costumes and lighting. I preferred the creative process. I had designed and sewn my own clothes in high school, dabbled in paint in fine art classes in college, and had watched the light on the ocean for years. I was ready. What they didn't tell me about being a theatre major was the very long days. I'd get up at sunrise. I'd jog or walk on the beach, sometimes swim, then shower and get to campus by 8 a.m. when the library opened. I'd spend the next three hours researching and studying. I'd walk through groves of eucalyptus trees to the theatre department where classes were held from noon to 6 p.m. It was then time to start work on the current assigned production. Rarely was I home before midnight.

My first production assignment was sound designer on a gangster play titled *The Petrified Forest*. I needed to find 1950s music, cars approaching and leaving, and the sound of gunshots. I'd record them onto a reel-to-reel tape. The sounds are spliced together with leader tape in order for the sound operator to know which sound is cued up next. In the "Sound Library" I found a record Father had once recorded: One side was the sounds of airplanes and the other the sound of trains. I laughed. He'd grown up the child of a live radio personality and knew each sound on those 1930s, 1940s, 1950s radio shows were produced by the sound engineer; shoes on a crate, a miniature door that made sound opening and closing, or coconut shells for horses walking.

Besides putting the sound effects' tape together I was also to be the sound operator. At dress rehearsal I had my reel-to-reel tape all cued up and ready to roll. Somewhere in the middle I missed a cue and a car was leaving when it should have been arriving.

The actors quickly responded to the situation with "Where did that car come from? I didn't hear it arrive."

I backed my tape up three cues only to have the gunshots go off when the car was supposed to be leaving. I failed as a sound operator, again.

The next show I worked on with my brother Jim. Jim was the set designer and a year ahead of me in the Theatre Design program. The play was Ibsen's *Lady from the Sea*. Jim designed a set using organic substances to create water, land and place. My job as stage assistant was to help find these elements. He wanted the flowers from the purple statice plant for water, sand for land and confetti for the rooms. The theatre department vetoed the use of sand, too messy and could harm the old wood floors. Jim chose eucalyptus leaves to replace the sand. A friend and I, under the guise of darkness, equipped with scissors and plastic bags, searched for the statice plants that flourish in the ocean climate. We filled three garbage bags. I dumped them onto my apartment floor to cut the blossoms from the stem when hundreds of earwigs ran for cover from the light. Great, *I love little bugs in my apartment*. The apartment was already filled with cockroaches. Jim spread his organic set elements onto the wood floor and it looked quite nice. What hadn't occurred to me was the fact there were to be three performances of this show. This meant either six more bags of statice (and earwigs) or after the show every night I would have to separate out the three elements. I chose the latter path, but it was time consuming. Nancy, the stage manager, volunteered to stay late and help. I brought out a bottle of Jack Daniels to reward our after-hours commitment. As we talked and laughed our way late into night, we realized this was the most ridiculous task any "design student" should have to endure—sorting purple statice blossoms from leaves and paper.

Long hours can fall into two categories, a short temper or giddy. Fortunately, I fell into the giddy category. I found having crushes on my professors and their assistants helped add some spark to the day. I had a crush on my polar opposite. He was in the graduate program with the goal of becoming a director. He had dark hair, rode a motorcycle and had a sharp cutting wit. He also had a girlfriend. I'd go ask his advice in the basement office he was given. If I was in one of my overwhelmed moods he had a bottle of Jack Daniels in a drawer that he'd generously share with an overworked undergraduate. He was East Coast and I was West Coast.

On New Year's Eve my roommate John suggested we take our dried-out Christmas tree down to the beach and set fire to it. I'd never done this before. It burned beautifully. We then strolled down the beach under a sky full of stars. We knew where some of the celebrities owned houses on Del Mar Beach and on the deck of one was Desi Arnaz, the husband on *I Love Lucy*. I was surprised he was alone on New Year's Eve. I wondered what price for fame he'd had to pay. I wanted to go up and talk to him as a fellow human being, but in the end respected his privacy.

My brothers had participated in the self-help seminar called EST (Erhard Seminars Training). They wanted me to take the two-day workshop. I'm not big on being told what to do and resisted. I thought they had probably been hypnotized and told to "tell your friends." They really kept insisting I take the next one scheduled in Los Angeles. They said I wouldn't be vulnerable enough if I took the workshop in San Diego. I guess they hadn't heard my stories from Europe. No, they weren't home when I returned and never asked. They told me not to book a hotel that someone would volunteer to take me home. Not that I'd ever been in that position before? Trying to find a stranger who'd let me sleep on their couch. I went. It was a large conference room. There were exercises in actuating authenticity. Looking into your inner thought processes. As lunchtime rolled around I recognized someone in the room. It was the father of an ex-high-school boyfriend. He invited me to join him for lunch. I'd been very fond of his son and enjoyed catching up on his whereabouts. The last time I'd seen his son, he was leaving to walk across the United States, coast to coast. His father informed me he had given up in the middle of the desert with blood blusters on his feet. Together we returned to the seminar.

Jim was correct; at the end of the day the organizers asked who needed lodging. I raised my hand. There were fewer volunteers to take us than expected. Eight of us went with one generous soul. I staked out a corner on her living room floor to sleep. The workshop continued the next day asking us to examine how we made decisions and were we taking responsibility for our choices. I suddenly "got it." For years I had been angry at the world for Father dying, and angry at a whale for sinking our boat. These things that happened weren't some overall grand scheme to punish me. I learned it is how I responded to the situation and not the situation itself that mattered. Okay, Jim, you were right, I needed this lesson. There was a graduation ceremony at the end. I looked back in the room and there were both my brothers. They had driven up from San Diego. I wasn't used to someone "being there." I was touched.

Technical theatre students were required to have a certain number of backstage production hours. I chose lighting as my design emphasis. There were three kinds of lights, called instruments, which we used. First was the Fresnel. It had a stepped Fresnel lens and gives a diffuse broad light. Next was the leko or ellipsoidal. This was a longer, heavier light that could narrow into a tight focus. Last was the spotlight that was used sparingly and needed someone to operate it during a production. The introduction course required we clean the instruments. We were to take them apart. Clean the glass lenses, check that the bulbs, called lamps, were working, and that all the bolts could easily be tightened and loosened. We also learned to change the connectors on the end. Some were still three-prong and could be pulled out accidentally. The better connection was a twist lock that made sure to stay plugged in. We stripped wires and then connected hot, neutral and ground to terminals. If there was extra cable we made extension cords.

For the third term I was master electrician. Richard Riddell, my lighting professor, was the lighting designer on the show. I was in charge of a crew of students to hang and focus the lights. Richard had gotten his doctorate in lighting design from Stanford and this was his first job after college. He came to the "hang" wearing Calvin Klein slacks, a white shirt and tie. Our theatre was a converted barn with wood beams across the ceiling on which pipes were attached. To hang a light one had to crawl on their stomach across the wood beams to where the light was to be positioned. From there a rope was thrown down both sides of the beam. The instrument would be tied to one end of the rope. The other rope end would be used to lift the light to the beam, similar to hoisting a sail. I wasn't about to let Richard get away without hanging some instruments and soon had him up on the beams. It was not a surprise when he came to the next day's "focusing session" in a t-shirt and jeans and even invited some of the crew to the campus pub for a pint afterwards.

Every student was required to bring a crescent wrench to tighten the C-clamp onto the metal pipe. Wrenches needed to be tied to their pants' belt loops in the rare case they fell, the wrench would not fall to the floor out of reach. I used a purple satin ribbon to tie my wrench to my jeans. The day the wrench slipped from my hand the satin ribbon's knot came undone and my wrench went slamming onto the theatre floor. The Technical Director thought about requiring everyone to start wearing hard hats, but didn't. It is difficult to look up at the ceiling for hours with a hard hat on.

Focusing the lights was tricky. That bright lamp that makes for great stage light heats up quickly. A technician has to work fast. There are a series of bolts that need to be tightened into place. There is a left and right swivel bolt and an up and down bolt. There is a knob that lengthens the beam of light if moved toward the stage or shortens the throw if pulled back. There are four shutters that can be adjusted to keep light from spilling into areas it isn't wanted. I'd come down from the beams with bruised hips, scorched hands and a rash from my proximity to the fiberglass insulation. More advanced theatres have catwalks that allow the technician to stand and walk from instrument to instrument. That theatre, the La Jolla Playhouse, was being built the year I graduated.

I was master electrician on a production being directed by Alan Schneider. Mr. Schneider was known for directing Broadway premieres of Edward Albee plays. The show he was directing for UCSD was a combination of three Thornton Wilder one-act plays. The last scene of the night has the actors dancing a waltz and encouraging the audience to join them. The master electrician's job is to run the light board during the show. This required I attend all rehearsals and performances. After one very late rehearsal my car, the TR3, wouldn't start. The last late night bus had just left. I sat on the curb in tears.

Alan Schneider came up and offered a hug while asking, "Do you need a ride home?"

I replied, "I called my roommate John who is coming to pick me up."

John sent his friend, Kirby, who had a crush on me. It was an awkward evening as exhaustion caught up with me, yet I had to pretend to be okay for both the director and Kirby. On closing night of the production Alan Schneider came up to the light booth to ask me for a waltz. I felt the bonding that theatre can create.

I had all the production credits I needed, but I volunteered in the costume shop. They had industrial sewing machines. I could zip through fabric as fast as Superman (no, he is DC Comics), as fast as Super Goof (that's better). The faculty costume designer often designed for the Oregon Shakespeare Festival. One of the records played in the costume shop was an Ashland singer songwriter by the name of Brian Freeman. Little did I know our paths would one day cross.

In the theatre department I often worked with Nancy. Our senses of humor meshed. We respected each other's intelligence and work ethic. Nancy was stage manager on most of the productions I crewed on. One of the "Introduction to Theatre" students, Jan, said she could get some magic mushrooms from her boyfriend in Ashland, Oregon, if anyone wanted some. I decided to heed Mother's words, "How can I judge something if I haven't tried it?"

I asked Nancy, "Would you be game for an adventure?"

She answered, "Yes."

A few weeks later Jan handed me a bag of dried mushrooms and said, "No charge."

Nancy and I needed to plan when and where. Spring Break was next week and the San Diego Zoo seemed a good destination. What we hadn't expected was how the mushrooms would enhance our imaginations. We walked from animal exhibit to exhibit and started recognizing our professors, family, friends in the faces and personality of the animals.

"Doesn't that kangaroo look just like Eric?" I exclaimed.

"Isn't that Koala Bear a little like Jorge?" Nancy replied.

We started laughing hysterically. We couldn't look anywhere without seeing someone we knew taking the shape of evolution in progress. Even Walt had once said, "There is nothing funnier than the human animal" or in our case the animal becoming human.

I was asked to design lights for a community theater production of *The Prime of Miss Jean Brodie*. It was being staged in a small converted theatre. This was pure volunteer and there were no stagehands to help. I went to the theatre one Sunday afternoon to focus the lights. I found a rickety old ladder and placed it between two rows of audience seating. It was at the top of this ladder I learned the danger of working with electricity. I plugged a lighting instrument into the socket and got a jolt of electricity through my body. I'm amazed I didn't fall off that ladder and lay in a deserted theatre for days until discovered. Faulty wiring is often a problem in old converted theatres.

I'd told many a boyfriend in high school and college I was not ready for sex until I had my own apartment. I was a little surprised when I moved back to Del Mar that some of these ex-boyfriends appeared at my door, even one from Colorado. I told each one of them they could stay one night, on the sofa, and that was as far as it was going to go. Did they really think I was going to keep my word?

One bright day I drove to the cliffs above Torrey Pines State Beach where the hang gliders took off. We'd owned a hang glider as teenagers, but I'd never gotten up the courage to actually jump off a cliff. I still wasn't up to that, but there were some lads flying airplane gliders. These seemed to be launched by an odd rubber band system.

One young man asked, "Would you like to join me in my glider?"

They seemed to be flying safely over the ocean and landing back on solid ground. What could go wrong?

I replied, "Yes."

I'm not really a thrill seeker, although I seemed to find myself in situations like this time after time.

His fellow friends pulled back the rubber band and off we went. What I found most remarkable, beside the view, was the quietness. It was extremely peaceful, with no engine noise I could take in the sounds of the sea, the wind, the sky as an open palette. We rode the air currents until the young pilot thought it best to head back to land. I thanked him for this unique and exhilarating experience. I headed down the road in the TR3 as my grandfather's white silk scarf, around my neck, fluttered in the wind.

My senior year of college I was behind in a few credits. I signed up for six classes the fall term, twenty-four credits (twelve to sixteen credits are normal). I soon found myself in a frenzy. The acting professor had asked us to choose one of our favorite objects to bring to class and tell why we picked that one. I couldn't do it. There were too many stories attached to what I owned. I didn't want to explain about the boat, about Father, and everything else seemed surface. I went to my advisor, Jorge Huerta. I adored Jorge. He'd been one of the instigators of the Chicano Theatre Movement. He sat me down and asked why I was in tears.

I said, "I just can't do it all. It is too much, especially the Acting II class. I can't even choose a stupid object."

He said, "Drop the class."

I said, "How? It is required for all theatre majors."

He said, "Well, those are the new rules. It wasn't required in the old rules. We'll go by the old rules for that class."

I was only partially relieved.

"I still need to take another term of a second language. I took French I in Colorado but not French II."

He thought about that for a minute as he looked at my transcript.

"Well," he said, "what is this Italian course you took in Florence?"

"I can count that?"

"Why not." Jorge just got promoted to sainthood. I then gave him the biggest hug ever and went lickity-split to the registrar's office to drop Acting II.

It was during the winter term that I walked by the theatre faculty offices and my lighting professor, Richard Riddell, popped his head out of his office.

He said, "I need you to go teach my first-year lighting students."

"What?!" I replied.

He said, "Just talk about your lighting design for *As You Like It*."

"Where is the class?"

"In the Mandeville Theatre."

"When?" I asked, a little worried.

"Now," he nonchalantly replied.

Great, I muttered to myself. I needed to get across campus and then stand in front of a bunch of students and talk. I have stage fright. But this would give me extra kudos points with my professor. And the Mandeville Theatre is where my lights were currently hung and focused for the production so I could do a "show and tell." Nothing like being put on the spot. Then, again, if he'd asked me the day before I would still have said yes, but not slept all night.

During spring term I was becoming more and more stressed about what I would be doing after college. Could I make a living with a theatre degree? I had stopped eating—stress seemed to do that to me. I called Mother panicked. I rarely called Mother for help, but I was eating two apples a day and throwing up the second one (bulimia) but really anorexia because how many people can feel guilty about eating two apples? Mother called our family doctor in Burbank who had treated Father.

Dr. Anderson could always fit me in during his lunchtime and insisted, "Come see me right away."

Dr. Anderson gave me an exam and then took me into his office to talk about my eating. He concluded I was anorexic. This wasn't a very publicized disorder at the time. He said I needed to see a therapist and he wanted me to see the best one in Hollywood who treated the movie stars. He made the appointment for me and I left his office. Two weeks later Mother flew my grandmother Eleanor out from Arkansas to accompany me to the therapist, a two-hour drive from San Diego. Great. With Grandma I have to pretend I am happy, and I don't really have any eating issues or other problems.

I walked into this upscale Hollywood therapist's office and as I entered he said, "I thought you'd be skinnier."

Well, gosh, geez, I guess that lets me off the hook. I'm not skinny enough so I don't have anorexia nor do I need a therapist. We did have our hour session. He concluded that I needed to see him on a weekly basis.

I disagreed. "No, thanks, I'm graduating college in a few weeks and don't know where I'll be living."

During the drive home Grandmother kept asking, "When are we going to stop for lunch?"

An apple, a fruit to be used in a pie, fed to a horse, eaten by a teacher, poisoned to prevent a potential princess from becoming queen. Apples became my life subsidence. When I had little time or desire to eat, it was an apple that would be my only food for the day. I found it ironic when my set design professor, Robert Israel, asked me to find "the perfect apple" to be photographed as an element of the set design we were working on. What is a perfect apple? I went from grocery store to grocery store trying to answer that question.

The day I graduated from UCSD Jeff was also graduating. I'd taken half a year off to go to Mexico and another half year to go to Europe. Jeff had stayed the course. My graduation ceremony was at UCSD's Muir College while Jeff's was at a UCSD's Fourth College, a different part of campus. As soon as I was handed my diploma, Mother, Sam, Eleanor and Jim headed to Jeff's ceremony. When my ceremony was over, I joined up with them. We all then headed to the Yacht Club. When we arrived, we saw smoke in the sauna and bathrooms building. It soon erupted into fire. Sam attempted to move the cars that were parked too close to the fire. Always good to celebrate momentous occasions with a little drama—we had front-row seats. The fire destroyed the building and it had to be rebuilt. We then enjoyed cocktails and lunch on the yacht club deck. Another milestone day filled with smoke and fire.

§

CHAPTER 30

Happily Ever After

My lighting design professor, Richard Riddell, was also my mentor and set me up for numerous lighting design interviews. I was flown to the San Francisco Opera to be interviewed for assistant lighting designer. I would have been hired if the assistant lighting designer I was to replace hadn't decided to return. Richard designed lights for the Oregon Shakespeare Festival. He told the master electrician, Robert (Bobby) Peterson, he should hire me. A week later I got a call from Bobby. We had a short interview on the phone and he said I had the job. Ashland, Oregon, it was to be. After working twelve-hour days throughout college, I was now going to be working twelve-hour days and get paid. This was honey on the toast. My salary was $600 a month.

Ashland was friendly and I was invited by a stranger to sleep on his couch until I could find my own apartment. I found a little furnished attic space a block from the theatre for $125 a month. I was rich. What I had yet to learn about Ashland was how hot the summers could be. 100 degrees hot and an attic apartment doesn't cool down until 2 a.m. Most of the Festival's cast and crew would frequent a French Restaurant after performances. The tourists would have spent the big money before the play. The restaurant gave Festival employees a discount and baskets of free bread. Around 2:30 a.m. I would head up the hill hoping my apartment had cooled enough to be able to sleep.

I liked most of my job. I was running the lighting control board for one production, working a slide projector on another, and switchboard on a third. Another element of a lighting technician's job was to make sure the lights don't fall and lose the spot where they were focused. Before every show each light is run through a light check. On the outdoor theatre this light check was done after the play, when it was dark.

The first day I asked the guys on the outdoor stage crew, "How do you get up the light tower to where the instruments are to be checked?"

Paul replied, "You climb the pole like a monkey."

If that is how the guys did it then that is how I was going to do it. It didn't take me but one minute to completely jam a toe backwards.

The other woman on the crew piped in, "I use the ladder. It is behind the curtains stage left."

Right. If only I had asked the guys to demonstrate for me how they climbed the pole first.

One show presented that summer was entitled *The Island* by Athol Fugard. It is set in a prison in South Africa. For this production the set designer wanted three monitors, TVs, the old kind, attached to the ceiling. Lighting instruments are heavy but lifting a TV up a rickety wooden ladder and over my head was hard work. I ordered some t-shirts made that read "Lights Not Videos," but I got no response to my subtle protest.

My last responsibility was changing the gels. These are thin, transparent dyed acetate that adds color to the otherwise white light. Every show had its own set of gels that had to be switched over. I liked to get up and do this early in the morning when there was no one else in the theatre. My days would start around 6 a.m. and end at midnight.

In Ashland I missed the ocean. It was a three-hour drive to the closest beach in Crescent City, California. My brother John had generously loaned me his Datsun 200SX for the summer. One bright sunny morning I didn't need to be at work until 7 p.m. I took advantage of my morning off to drive to the beach. The drive was windy and goes through the majestic Redwood State Park. I walked on the beach and smelled the ocean breeze. When I was ready to return, I looked at my map of Oregon and saw there was a more direct road back. As many before me have learned, these roads are not really roads. They are made for logging trucks, and not maintained or paved. Ignorantly, I took off on this "quicker" drive home. There were corners where I feared I might run into a logging truck. There were places where I looked down extremely steep cliffs, into the Rogue River, and wished I'd never looked at that map. It was a five-hour drive of pure panic.

A few weeks later I was invited to what I considered a mandatory crew party at my boss, Bobby's house, in Trail, Oregon. It was a hot day and I'd made a date for later that night with Harry back in Ashland. Bobby's house was an unfinished log cabin.

When I inquired, "Where is the bathroom?" Bobby pointed to the trees up the hill. To an ex-San Diego Yacht Club girl this was not funny. Bobby wasn't kidding. Everyone else was down at the creek, naked, in a deep swimming hole. After a few hours I was ready to leave, when Bobby and his best friend Brian, a folk musician, came down from the house with a bottle of Jack Daniels.

They asked, "Want to join us upstream?"

"Fine," I said.

Except for the crayfish that startled me, sitting on a rock in the creek was refreshing. After that there were horseshoes with every ringer getting a drink of Jack. I was getting lots of ringers.

Everyone was leaving and I was ready to go as well when Bobby pulled out a deck of cards and said, "Anyone up for poker?"

I can't think of a time I wasn't up for a game of cards. I was practically weaned on odds, counting cards and probability, and I was cleaning up.

I headed outside to use the facilities when Brian came out.

"There is no way you are driving back, in the dark, on those twisty mountain roads," Brian exclaimed while taking my car keys.

I spent the night outside on the dog's sofa with Brian and lots of burrs.

I had stood up Harry in Ashland.

The next day Brian left flowers at my apartment door. I never turned over the card to see he'd also invited me out.

It didn't take long for him to call and say, "Can I take you to breakfast tomorrow?"

"That would be wonderful," I replied. He did not show up until 1 p.m. I'd been waiting since 7 a.m. This was breakfast time in a musician's world.

Our next date sealed my motto: "Humor in Adversity." The weather had been over 100 degrees and we were headed back to Bobby's creek to swim. We made it to the Medford off ramp, twenty miles up the road, when his car stopped. It just died. We spent the day in the gas station asphalt parking lot trying to figure out how to fix his car. There were many trips across the street and a long hotter parking lot to a hardware store where tools were bought and tried and failed. When the time came I had to be at work, he called a friend who could tow us back to Ashland. As soon as the car started to be towed it turned over and we could drive home. This was not my favorite date.

In November 1981 my theatre contract was up. I had decided to head back to San Diego. Mother invited Brian and me to Thanksgiving at her house in Boulder City, Nevada. I accepted. The cost to fly was prohibitive. Brian's old VW van would never make it that far. I'd given my brother John back his car. The cheapest way to get to Mom's house was for me to buy a used car. I found a Subaru for $600 that we thought was a great purchase. We were told it had a small oil leak. We stopped a half dozen times on the trip to check the oil.

Each time Brian declared, "The oil looks good to me."

We spent the night in Reno. The next day two hours down the road Brian discovered he had left his wallet in the hotel room (not really that important since he didn't have any money in it). A half hour later the car started to stutter, a loud sound was heard from the engine. The car slowly stopped at the side of the road outside the town of Fallon, Nevada. Upon lifting the hood Brian noticed that the car had thrown a rod. It was out of oil. Hadn't Brian been checking the oil? Brian had been checking the transmission fluid, not the oil. Okay, now what? We found a mechanic who'd tow the car to his shop. He gave me an estimate of $1,000 to replace the engine block. He assured me that once this was done, I would have a practically new car.

I replied, "Replace the engine."

We still had to get to Boulder City where Mother now lived. There was a bus to Las Vegas that left at midnight. We had 12 hours to kill. Our first stop was the local library to investigate what history this small Nevada town had to offer—not much. There was a movie theatre and a movie we hadn't seen. The main attraction in town was the casino. We decided to try one slot machine. It only took Silver Dollars and we only had one. The name of the slot machine was "Friday the 13th." That fit our mood. We put our silver dollar in the slot and pulled the lever—three flat tires in a row! We must have won! It would have been a large payout if we'd put in three silver dollars, but one dollar bought us nothing. We finally succumbed to the bar and ordered a beer. We started writing a song about this long day. The "New Fallon Waltz" was written, edited and finalized. Exhausted, we headed to the bus at 11:30 p.m. and Mother Nature had another trick up her sleeve as it started to snow. And I really don't like cold. The bus finally arrived and as we handed over our tickets we discovered it was completely full—no two seats together. At dawn we arrived in Las Vegas. My stepfather Sam was there to pick us up for the 45 minute drive to Boulder City.

Mother and Sam had bought a Spanish stucco house on a hill overlooking Lake Mead. Mother was cooking dinner. What did she do? She cooked Coquille Saint Jacques (scallops in a wine cream sauce). Here we had gone through this whole ordeal on Catalina Island about tradition and turkey and I brought my new boyfriend home only to find out that tradition didn't count anymore? Fortunately, Brian loves scallops, and thought this was the best Thanksgiving dinner anyone could wish for. That night Brian proposed marriage and gave me a masking tape ring with a diamond drawn on it. My plans of returning to the beaches of Del Mar suddenly dissolved.

Mother had teased me growing up. She said I could not marry until I had sewn seven quilts. This must be a traditional left over from the Oregon Trail days when you really needed seven quilts to stay warm in the winter with no central heating. I loved designing and sewing quilts. I enjoyed the intricacy of choosing compatible fabrics, cutting them into geometric shapes and sewing them together to create new patterns by their juxtaposition. With the addition of batting to turn the flat fabric into a fluffy warm blanket. I had definitely made more than seven quilts required by this Thanksgiving, although I'd given most away as presents.

Back in Ashland we found a wedding ring in a downtown antique store. It was a small diamond with two rubies on each side. My birthstone is diamond and Brian's is ruby. Brian was performing five nights a week at restaurants and pubs for little money, but there was a tip jar. I considered putting a $100 bill into that wine carafe tip jar to pay for the ring, but worried someone might steal it. Instead, as many musicians are prone to do, Brian borrowed the money for the ring from his mother.

We had a simple wedding at Mother's house in Boulder City, Nevada. I bought a 1890s lace blouse I'd admired in an Ashland antique shop. I sewed a simple white cotton skirt to wear with it. We found Brian a tux jacket and shirt in another antique store. He was considering wearing jeans, but switched to gray slacks at the last minute. He braided his long hair down his back tying a gray satin ribbon to the end of the braid. The flowers were simple: Daisies and baby's breathe. Many family and friends made the journey to the middle of the desert to honor and witness our marriage ceremony.

My grandmother Helen whispered in my ear right before the ceremony, "Never marry a musician."

Now she tells me.

Even though my husband to be was a musician, I wrote our wedding song:

"Once upon a time, when I was younger than today,
I waited for my Prince to come, And take me far away.
Paper rings we exchanged, with diamonds painted on,
A promise of forever to make each other strong.
Dreams become reality with the morning light,
and the long-lost Princess still marries the gallant knight."

§

CHAPTER 31

Where is That Magic Wand When You Need It?

When I got married, I psychologically felt that was the end of my "childhood" and beginning of "adulthood." In the next thirty years Brian and I bought and paid off a house. We raised two intelligent, honest, and creative children. We established our own graphic arts business, Crystal Castle Graphics. My husband could draw anything and at one time entertained the concept of applying to Disney as an animator. The art studio was out of our house allowing my husband and me to work side-by-side and be home for our two children/teenagers/young adults. We loved our work and our clients. We've accomplished Walt's philosophy, "When your work is your passion, you don't work for money."

2008 was the year I was turning fifty. Something about this birthday made me anxious. It wasn't about gray hairs. I didn't have any. I planned a party for 18 guests, as many as our small house could seat. I made a list of which friends would enjoy "playing games." Actors, musicians and teachers were invited. I gave away poker chips throughout the night to be used on a roulette wheel for prizes. I was trying to turn the table—"Don't bring me presents; I'm giving them to you." The prizes included a quilt I'd sewn, a Barnes and Noble gift card, a few bottles of Jack Daniels (since it was really Jack who responsible for our marriage), and other symbolic items. The night was a success.

In May, a month after my birthday, there was a planned Sherman Children Reunion on the island of Molokai to celebrate Mother's 75th birthday a few months earlier. The four adult Sherman children rented condos. These condos were next to the old Sheridan Hotel Golf Course. In recent years the hotel had been abandoned. The golf course had not been watered. The resort was falling into decay. The sundry shop was still open with its small supply of essentials: Snacks, soda and beer. Dinners were with Mom and Sam. The days were ours to swim, hike or relax on the beach.

There was a hike planned to one of our favorite coves to snorkel. I'd hiked to this cove on an earlier trip at dawn without much effort. This day we left at noon and the sand and lava rocks were hot. I found myself dizzy. Not the dizzy I was used to from not eating, but the type of dizzy that made me think I might faint, and fall off the cliff into the turquoise Molokai Ocean. My brother Jim was great at allowing me a slower pace and helping me up the steeper trails. The cove was brilliant. We snorkeled. I saw a sunken boat and many vibrant fish: Butterfly, parrot, and trigger. Out beyond the waves I spotted a sea turtle. Jeff reported seeing an octopus. I had not brought lunch, I hadn't thought to. I had brought water. Jim split his peanut butter sandwich with me. The return walk was an easier trail through grasslands. Once back at the condo I felt very weak and in need of a nap.

Upon returning to Ashland I found myself crawling from sofa to bed to sofa. My husband threatened to call my doctor if I didn't. I made an appointment. Blood tests showed I was severely anemic. An endoscopy was ordered and a tumor with a bleeding ulcer on it was found in my stomach. Surgery was scheduled. Half of my stomach was removed with the tumor.

My surgeon and doctor both said, "Don't worry, the tumor was benign."

To a child who grew up hearing, "Your father's fine, the tumor was benign," it is hard to rest assured that one tumor is all I'm ever going to have although I'm not a fatalist type of person.

I started reading about my tumor, WildGIST, a very rare cancer. From my research I learned there was a dyad for WildGIST and paraganglioma, Father's and Aunt Ann's cancer. There is a DNA mutation that if present indicates a genetic link. After two years of waiting for DNA testing results, I learned I did have a mutation in the SDHB gene. I had inherited Father's cancer. Thanks, Dad. There is still no cure. The SDHB gene is involved in the Krebs Cycle, responsible for turning food into energy. Couldn't this mutation have reinforced, if not caused my anorexia? If food isn't being properly absorbed, why eat?

The cost of surgery was beyond my savings account and as I considered where I could come up with $10,000 I realized the only thing in our house that I might be able to sell for that much money was an original oil paining of Uncle Scrooge by Carl Barks. Carl had given Father this painting as a thank-you present. This painting I had taken to college with me. It was my subliminal connection to Father. Then it occurred to me the irony of having to sell Scrooge to pay for a tumor that I also inherited from Father. I put the painting up for auction at the Heritage Auction House. It wasn't an easy decision and I sent at least fifty emails to my consigner, David. A similar painting had sold for $50,000. That amount would pay for this surgery and future medical needs. The day of the auction the European Stock Market crashed and the painting went for $20,000 ($15,000 to me). It took me only a day to realize the painting was a thing and it had brought in the money I needed. No reason to be greedy and wish for more. What I hadn't expected from this transaction were the number of people who contacted me having known Father and shared their kind words with me thirty-five years after his death. This was much more important than owning a painting. I had found my "money bin" in the gift of other's stories about Father and their respect for his work, his intelligence and his humor.

I hadn't lost all connections with the studio. Roy Disney, Jr., had written me letters at Christmas for years. I had received a handwritten note from him three weeks before he died of cancer in 2009. I hadn't known he was ill. He was giving me his condolences on Mother's recent passing.

What does one do when they hear they have a malignant cancer? In my case I started researching all the top doctors in the world. Most would email me back within a day with what their research was finding. Doctors at the National Cancer Institute were extremely open about their research going as far as offering to fly me to Maryland for one of their semi-annual conferences on this disease. To date there isn't a known drug that helps with the tumors, although many are being tested. Their medical protocol is to scan for tumors twice a year with the hope if the tumors are found small enough, surgery can be performed. Besides, as Uncle Remus sang, *"You can't run away from trouble—there ain't no place that far."*

My new health reality involves driving five hours to Portland, Oregon, where the head doctor in Oregon on this cancer practices. Twice a year numerous tests, including CT scans, are scheduled. During these tests dye is injected into my blood. Also injected into my blood was my need to tell this story. Revisiting a father who died before his time. My own transition from innocently floating on ocean waves to having iodine-filled IVs in my veins. My need to talk about the impact a pivotal death has on those left behind. I wanted to write about the strength and vulnerability that comes from being a survivor. Passing on the medical and emotional knowledge obtained from being born into one-in-a-million circumstances.

If I could find and pull that Sword out of the Stone would I be ordained a different future? If I traded back the Tomboy for a Long-Lost Princess would it come with a Fairy Godmother? Did I miss my chance? Did I fall asleep too early the night I could have "Wished Upon a Star"? Did I get off the train one stop before the Wishing Well? I have three brothers and DNA mutations are a 50-50 chance of being passed onto the children. Did my need to always be first change my probability of getting Father's cancer? Did it have to choose the only girl?

You'd think with all the powers on my side—Tinkerbell, Mad Madame Mim, Merlin, Super Goof, Three Good Fairies; Flora, Fauna and Merryweather, the Seven Dwarfs, and even Mary Poppins—I would have some power to change my future. Maybe it is time to make up a new portion: 1 tablespoon Pixie Dust, 2 teaspoons Supercalifragilisticexpialidocious, 3 parts First Kiss, 1 owl feather, a dash of innocence, a sliver of moonlight, stir and simmer. Drink only from the hands of a Prince Charming. Can I put all my chips on that long shot of a cure? The cards I was dealt. Fortunately, I have always been up for a game of poker.

§

Afterword

Surrendering to the Beast

I'd like to say when the tumors come for me that I've lived my life to the fullest. Appreciated my unique and privileged childhood. Explored the world in my young adult years with curiosity and an open mind. Laughed and cried appropriately. Kept a bit of the fantasy world of comic books in my back pocket. Listened to the squirrels and trees talking to each other. Taught my children solid Disney values: Trust, respect, honesty and humor, with the intention they will venture forth and inspire others. And, last, wished my father could have edited this book for me. He was a great man.

§

Acknowledgments

I was given the use of a magic wand three times in my life. The first was being born into a family with a father and mother who were creative, intelligent, kind, funny, and loved children.

The second time was when our boat sank. There was someone close by to literally take their hands, pull them out of the life raft, and delivery them back to me. The irony being only "my mother" could find a whale sleeping in the middle of the ocean and hit it.

The third was finding my husband, Brian, in a small town in Oregon, who had my father's sarcasm, sense of humor, artistic abilities, musical aspirations, honesty and devotion to family.

A Disney Childhood began when I learned I had inherited my father's cancer. I began writing about my childhood and how important Father's sense of humor was to my upbringing. As a child I lived in this comic book world where anything could happen and I was always on the lookout for the comic twist in any given situation. I learned to laugh my way through the absurdities of this world and adopted the motto *Humor in Adversity*. I wasn't exactly counting on as much adversity as came my way, but I had been given the tools to fight back and then find some shred of irony to make me laugh.

I couldn't have written this story without the many individuals who mentored me, told me stories, read my rough drafts (and they were rough), and strangers who simply said, "I want to read your book." I truly appreciate the tellers at my bank, and grocery cashiers who'd hear a segment of book one week at a time and encouraged me on with their laughter and genuine interest that my book got published.

I never have given my husband, Brian Freeman, enough credit. He has always encouraged me no matter what asinine idea I'd have come up with this time. He has stood beside me (literally since we've worked together in the same an 8 x 10 room for 30 years) in every idea I've put forth. There isn't a day that goes by that at some point we find ourselves laughing hysterically at some twisted thought that has occurred to us simultaneously.

I give credit to my two children who've had to live with this crazy mom for years, never knowing when I was teasing (I always was), but as adults have learned how to slam my attempts at sarcasm right back into my court and ace me.

Diana Maul is the best friend I've never met. We've emailed back and forth for ten years and she has put in hundreds of hours copyediting this book without ever wanting anything in return except to see it published.

My father's Disney colleagues, and friends, whom when I randomly, thirty-five years after his death, sent them a letter, "Did you know my father?" all responded with, "Your father was my best friend and let me know how I can help." This included his London colleague Peter Woods and his wife Barbara, who also took me in during my college years. Peter mailed me photos and told me stories about what happened when you travelled with Father. Wendall Mohler, Father's American colleague, told me some outrageous stories and was encouraging from the start that I had something definitely worth reading. Freeman Gosden, Jr., who gave my story rave reviews as well as great criticism. He told me stories about Father's teenage years. Father's friends from Pomona, Bruno Salmon, and his wife Billie Jean, who read my manuscript and gave me solid feedback. Tom Golberg and his wife Louise, who were very close to Father during his twenty years at Disney, and encouraged me to write. I thank their daughter, Karen, who took on the job as email correspondent. Carson van Osten, whom Father hired as an illustrator straight out of college and later took over part of Father's job when he died. Carson answered my numerous emails full of questions and more questions.

There were numerous Disney historians who offered help and advice. Didier Ghez was one of the first to read the manuscript and suggested ways I could enrich the story and gave me the name of Ben Ohmart, a publisher, he thought would be the perfect venue for my story. The other writers and historians who emailed and called with sources were: David Gerstein, Michael Barrier, Germund von Wowern, Mark Evanier, Dana Gabbard (who put Father on Wikipedia), Alberto Becaltini in Italy and Roy Disney, Jr., who has passed away but who wrote me for years enforcing my belief that Disney was family.

I want to thank my brothers John, Jim and Jeff who all contributed in some way, whether it was a memory, editing, or finding old photos in the attic. I also feel privileged to have grown up with such imaginative siblings who were willing to let me tell our story. My mother, unfortunately, has passed away, but her presence is in the book with her wonderful journal description of *Atorrante's* sinking.

I am indebted to Nick Frazee who rescued my mother, brothers and our crew from the little rubber raft. Nick told me, "Your mother was the smartest, prettiest woman I've ever picked up in the middle of the Pacific." His re-entry into my life, when I asked if he might have a photo I could use, has been another unexpected gift the writing of this book has brought me.

There were numerous girlfriends who literally held my hand and helped dry my tears through my teenage years. A special hug to Janice, Lisa, Nancy and my dormmates at Colorado College. And Lisa's whole family, The Welshes, who came to my rescue many a time, fed me Sunday brunches and said "I'll never be an orphan while they are alive."

I thought when I had to sell the Carl Barks oil painting of "Uncle Scrooge" I was losing a part of my connection to father. Instead, I got something far greater than money in that exchange. I received numerous warm memories about Father, and his contribution to Disney's comic book program, as well as his kindness to others, that hasn't been forgotten. Through the selling of the painting the concept to write this story emerged.

The other side of this coin is my diagnosis of cancer. It has introduced me into another world of individuals in my same circumstances. Louise, part of my cancer support group, took my manuscript seriously and spent hours helping me polish the synopsis, which, only 30 minutes after submitting, to just one publisher, I had a "YES." I want to give a big hug to the kids and adults fighting the Wildgist/Paraganglioma Dyad and Triad. They are an inspiring group researching and educating others about this rare cancer. I am especially in awe of Erin MacBean, whose knowledge of paraganglioma is tremendous, and her ability to communicate it to others is a gift to us all. This praise also goes to the other writers of the newsletter "Paratroopers." I've encounter many informative doctors at the National Cancer Institute who take hours to talk to every new diagnosed patient, who are often panicked, and given them straight forward knowledge of this disease and everything they've accumulated to date, especially Dr. Su Young Kim. There is also my doctor in Portland, who took me on, Dr. Heinrich, a dedicated expert on GIST cancers. My life is blessed.

§

About the Author

Cathy Sherman Freeman was born in the 1950s, one short block from Disney Studios, where her father was Head of Publications. Her childhood involved entertaining Disney foreign representatives who'd travelled to Burbank. They were the "Typical American Family" and escorted these guests to Disneyland.

Cathy grew up with a great respect for all cultures and core values based on Disney ideals with a comic book twist. She attended Colorado College for two years as an English major before travelling to Europe for nine months. She transferred to the University of California, San Diego and graduated magna cum laude in theatrical design.

Her first job, as a lighting technician, was at the Oregon Shakespeare Festival in Ashland, Oregon. There she met her husband and stayed. They combined their artistic skills and for thirty years have worked side-by-side as graphic designers in an art studio to the side of their house. They were two parents "home" to raise two smart, imaginative and sarcastic children.

Visit Cathy on the Web at www.ADisneyChildhood.com.

Index

Ford, Sam - 7, 136, 145, 150, 154
France - 7, 14, 24, 25, 121
Francis, Blair - 85
Frazee, Nick - 85, 94, 95, 96, 99
Freeman, Brian - 88, 129, 130, 142, 148, 149, 150, 151, 153
Frog Shop, The - 41

G

G.I. Journal - 8, 82
Geisha dancer - 25, 78
Gentleman's Agreement - 9
German officer - 25, 38
Germany - 10, 24, 37, 80, 131, 138
Golberg, Tom - 13
Gold Key Comics - 4
Goofy - 3, 14, 48, 50, 99
Gosden, Jr., Freeman - 9
Gould, Gary - 85
Granger, Joy - 75
Grant, Cary - 9
Green Lantern Restaurant - 37
grunions - 72

H

Haines, Bob - 85
Halloween - 49, 102
halter-tops - 72, 73, 137
halyard - 98, 104, 105
Hamley's Toy Store - 37
Hampton Court - 36
Hanging Tree, The - 58
Harald the Fine Hair - 7
Harcourt, Hastings - 104, 105
Hogan, David - 88
Holland - 37, 49
Hope, Bob - 8
Hope, Chuck - 85
hopscotch - 24
Hotel Borth -127
Houdini - 11
Huerta, Jorge - 143
Hussongs - 99

I

I Love Lucy - 9, 140
Innsbruck, Austria - 40
Island, The - 130, 148
Isle of Wight - 125
Isomata - 59
Israel, Robert - 145
It's a Small World - 16
It's Magic - 11
Italy - 14, 35, 39, 40, 80, 118,

J

Japan - 2, 9, 12, 14, 15, 19, 20, 21, 25, 44, 47, 48, 78
Johnston, O.B. - 13, 54, 55, 83, 116
Jungle Book, The - 5, 30, 35, 37, 39, 79

K

Kauai - 96
Kendrick, Dick & Polly - 111, 112
Kick-the-Can - 27
Kimball, Ward - 20
kimono - 48, 78
Kirschner, Fred - 85
kite - 33, 98, 104
Koblischek, Horst - 80
kumquat - 20-21

L

La Dow, Jerry - 85
Lady from the Sea - 123, 139
Lamour, Dorothy - 8, 82
Laugh-In - 15
Lewis and Clark College - 67-68, 71
Little Golden Books - 4
London - 14, 35, 36, 37, 39, 40, 50, 53, 75, 79, 80. 117, 123, 124, 125, 129, 130

V

Van de Velde, B. - 80
Vanneste, Andre - 80
Venezuela - 54
Venice - 39
Victoria and Albert Museum - 36

W

Walker, Card - 54, 116
Wayne, John - 20
Welsh, Lisa - 70, 72, 73-74, 88, 93, 94, 99, 108
Western Publishing - 4
whale - 95, 96, 140
Whistle Wing V - 104, 105
Wildtype GIST - 154
William the Conqueror - 7
Wonderful World of Disney Magazine - 48-49
Wonderful World of Disney Television Show - 4, 28
Wonders of the Jungle - 28
Woods
      Peter - 14, 36, 75, 80, 129, 130
      Barbara - 36, 80, 129, 130
World War II - 2, 8, 10, 36, 82, 131, 132

Y

Yokoyama, Matsuo - 178
You're a Good Man Charlie Brown - 61
Yugoslavia - 14, 15, 40

Z

Zagreb - 40
zits - 38, 54
Zuma - 61

Note: This book's photo section has been reviewed by TWDC Image Licensing and some photos have been removed per request of the Studio.

CPSIA information can be obtained at www.ICGtesting.com
Printed in the USA
BVOW010828170512

290452BV00003B/2/P